Eighteen Songs
of a Nomad Flute

EIGHTEEN SONGS OF A NOMAD FLUTE

胡笳十八拍

THE STORY OF LADY WEN-CHI

A FOURTEENTH-CENTURY HANDSCROLL IN THE METROPOLITAN MUSEUM OF ART

INTRODUCTION,
COMMENTARY, AND
TRANSLATION OF POEMS
BY ROBERT A. ROREX
AND WEN FONG

The Metropolitan Museum of Art
Distributed by New York Graphic Society

LIBRARY OF CONGRESS CATALOGING IN PUBLICATION DATA

Main entry under title:
Eighteen songs of a nomad flute: the story of Lady Wen-chi.

The text of the poems on the scroll reproduced here is by Liu Shang; the paintings are by an unknown artist.

1. Liu Shang, 8th cent. Hu chia shih pa p'ai—Illustrations. 2. Painting, Chinese—Sung-Yuan dynasties, 960–1368. 3. New York (City). Metropolitan Museum of Art. 4. Ts'ai, Yen, ca. 177–ca. 239—Art. I. Rorex, Robert A., ed. II. Fong, Wen, ed. III. Liu, Shang, 8th cent. Hu chia shih pa p'ai. English. 1974. IV. New York (City). Metropolitan Museum of Art.
ND3399.L55E37 759.951 74-11140

Introduction

The paintings and poems reproduced here are those of a handscroll acquired by The Metropolitan Museum of Art in 1973 from the collection of Chi-ch'ien Wang as a Gift of the Dillon Fund. The height of the scroll is 11⅜ inches; the length of the longest scene, the fourteenth, is 32 inches. A description of the scroll and its colophons and collectors' seals has already been published.[1] Some of the seals are reproduced on the cover of the present book.

The daughter of Ts'ai Yung, a scholar-statesman of the Han dynasty, Lady Wen-chi was abducted from her father's home in Ch'en-liu, in present-day Honan, about A.D. 195.[2] Taken by her captors, the Southern Hsiung-nu (identical with the Huns who later invaded Europe), into Inner Mongolia, she was made the wife of the *tso hsien wang*, the commander in chief of the nomad tribe's left wing. Years passed before a ransom mission found her. The lady now faced a painful choice: to remain with her husband and children in the harsh and alien land that she detested, or to give up this family and return to her own people.

Wen-chi's decision to return to China became associated with some cherished ideas: the superiority of Chinese civilization over the cultures beyond her borders, the irreconcilability of the different ways of life; the necessity for the individual to bear the burdens thrust upon one by fate; and, above all, the Confucian concept of loyalty to one's ancestral family and state.

The lady's story has been told and retold in China. Wen-chi herself is credited with the earliest contributions to the literature about her: she is said to be the author of two extended poems, called "Laments," that are appended to her biography in the *History of the Latter Han Dynasty*, compiled about A.D. 440, as well as a cycle of poems known as the *Eighteen Songs of a Nomad Flute*.[3] A later cycle of *Eighteen Songs* was written by Liu Shang of the T'ang dynasty, about 773, and still another cycle was written by the Northern Sung statesman Wang Anshih (1021–86).

It was Liu Shang's cycle[4] that received the most important pictorial treatment. Among the masterpieces of Chinese painting in the Museum of Fine Arts, Boston, are four badly damaged album leaves collectively

Painting for the third poem.
The Museum of Fine Arts, Boston

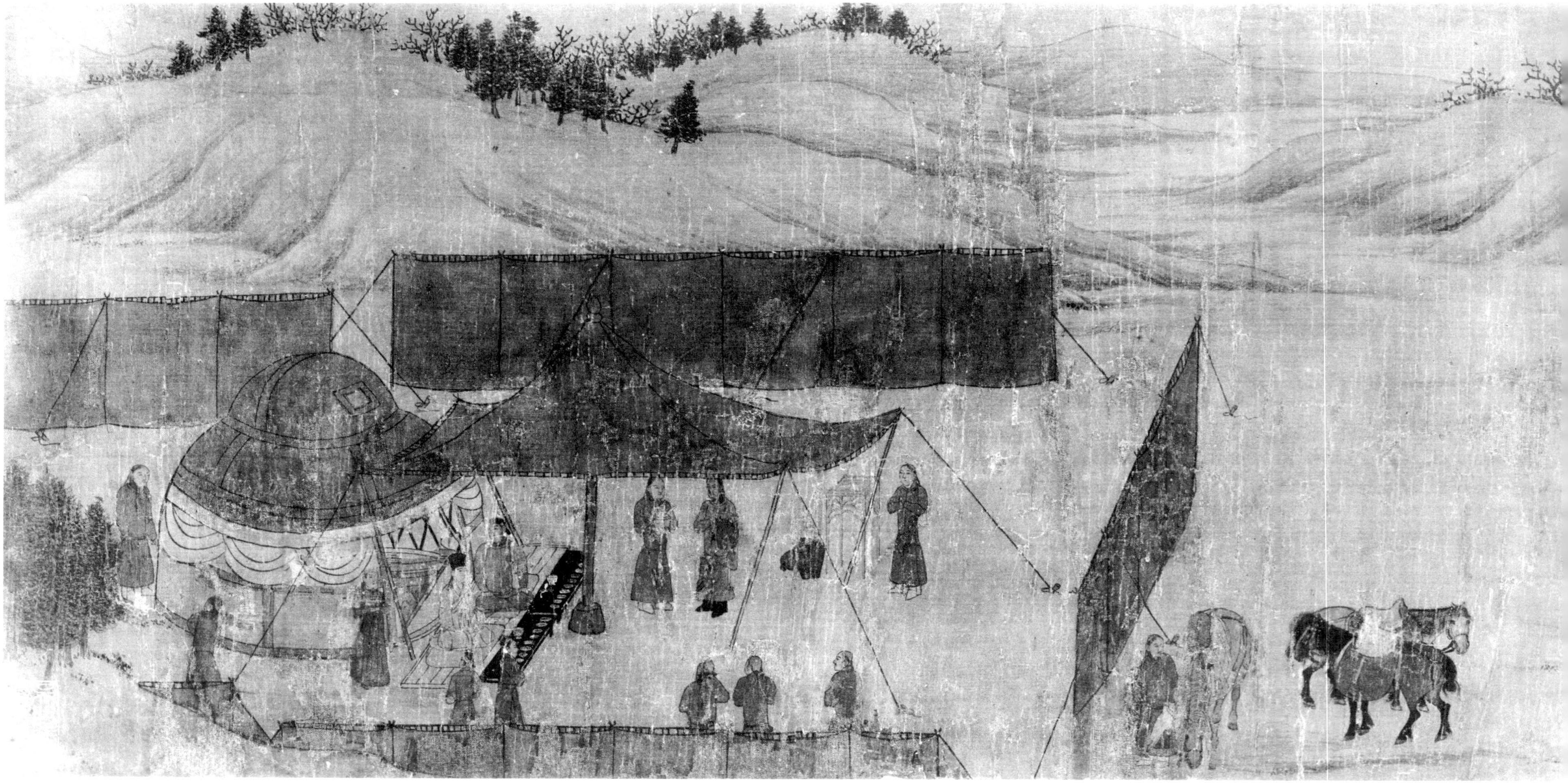

known as "Wen-chi's Captivity in Mongolia and Her Return to China." It is evident that these twelfth-century paintings are fragments of a handscroll that once included eighteen pictures illustrating Liu Shang's poems.

Of the surviving copies of the original paintings,[5] the Metropolitan Museum's handscroll comes closest to providing us with the look of the originals. It is the oldest of the copies, and when one compares it with the Boston paintings it proves to be an almost exact copy. Though it is difficult to date this kind of work precisely, the quality of the drawing

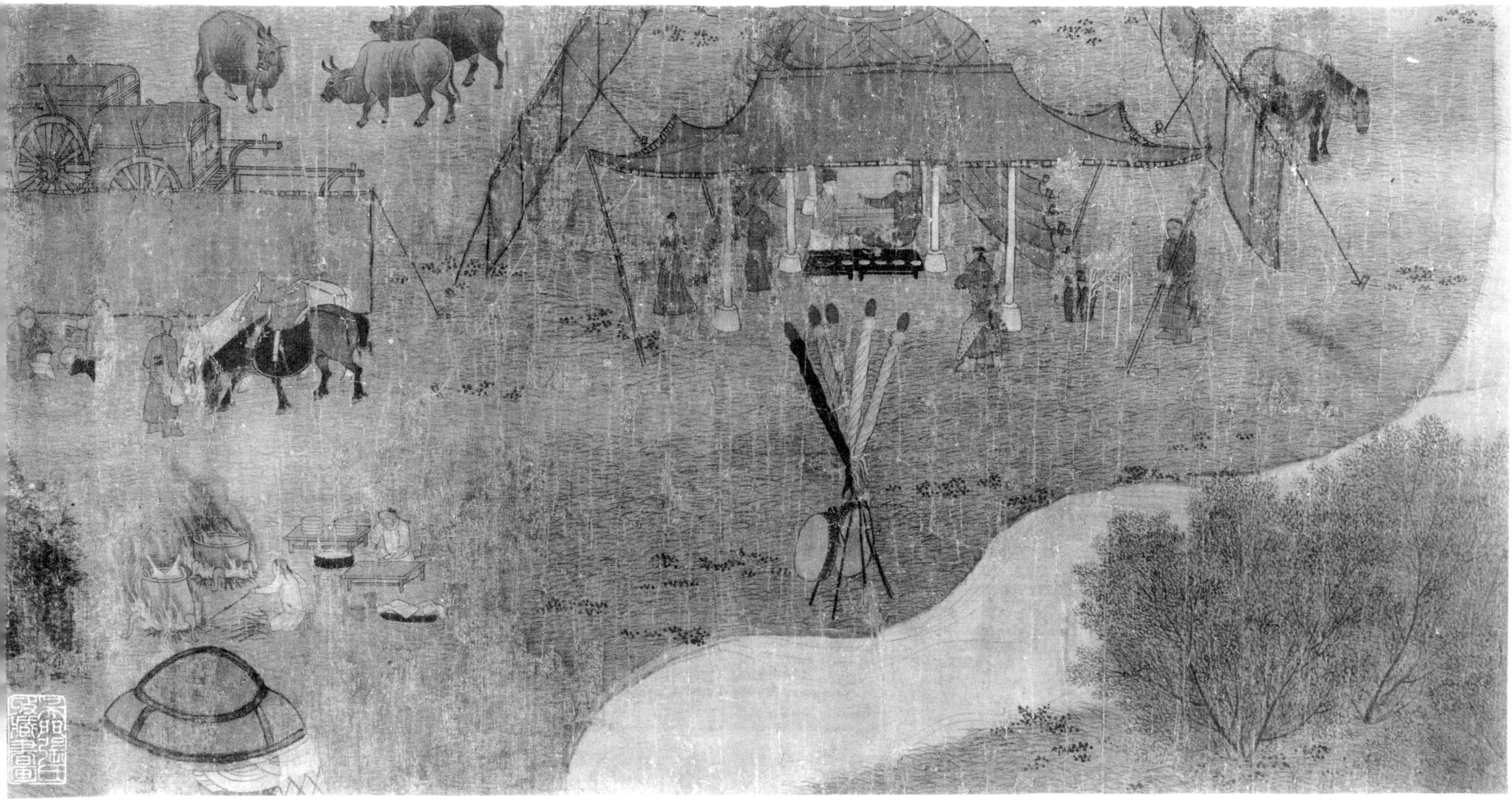

Painting for the fifth poem.
The Museum of Fine Arts, Boston

suggests that the Metropolitan Museum's copy was not made before the fourteenth century. This is roughly confirmed by the oldest of the many collectors' seals on the scroll: those of the Mu family of the early fifteenth century. (The identification of an earlier seal, that of Chia Ssu-tao [died 1275] is questionable.)

The calligraphy of the poems does not help much with the dating. It is in the familiar *k'ai-shu* style of Kao-tsung, the first emperor of the Southern Sung dynasty (reigned 1127–61): a slightly archaized regular script showing parallel horizontal strokes in a square formation. The idiosyncracies of Kao-tsung's style are accurately preserved, but now and then certain strokes, especially the final wavelike *na,* seem unnatural, and a few of the characters appear wobbly. By transilluminating the scroll we are able to see that some of the strokes are meticulously outlined and then filled in, rather than written freehand. In other words, the calligraphy appears to be a tracing.

We are certain that the original cycle of paintings made to illustrate

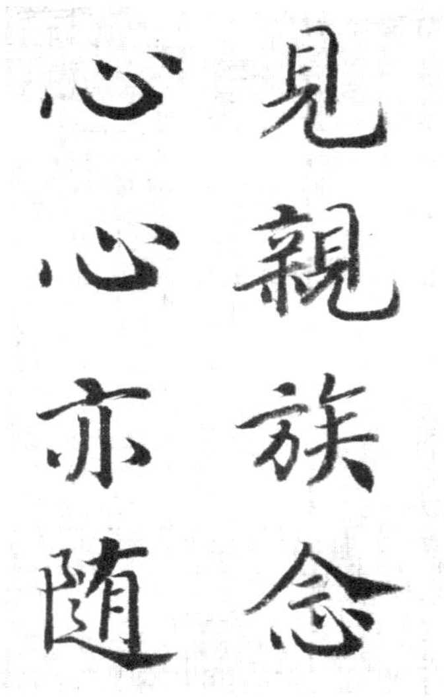

Sample of the calligraphy, the fourteenth poem.

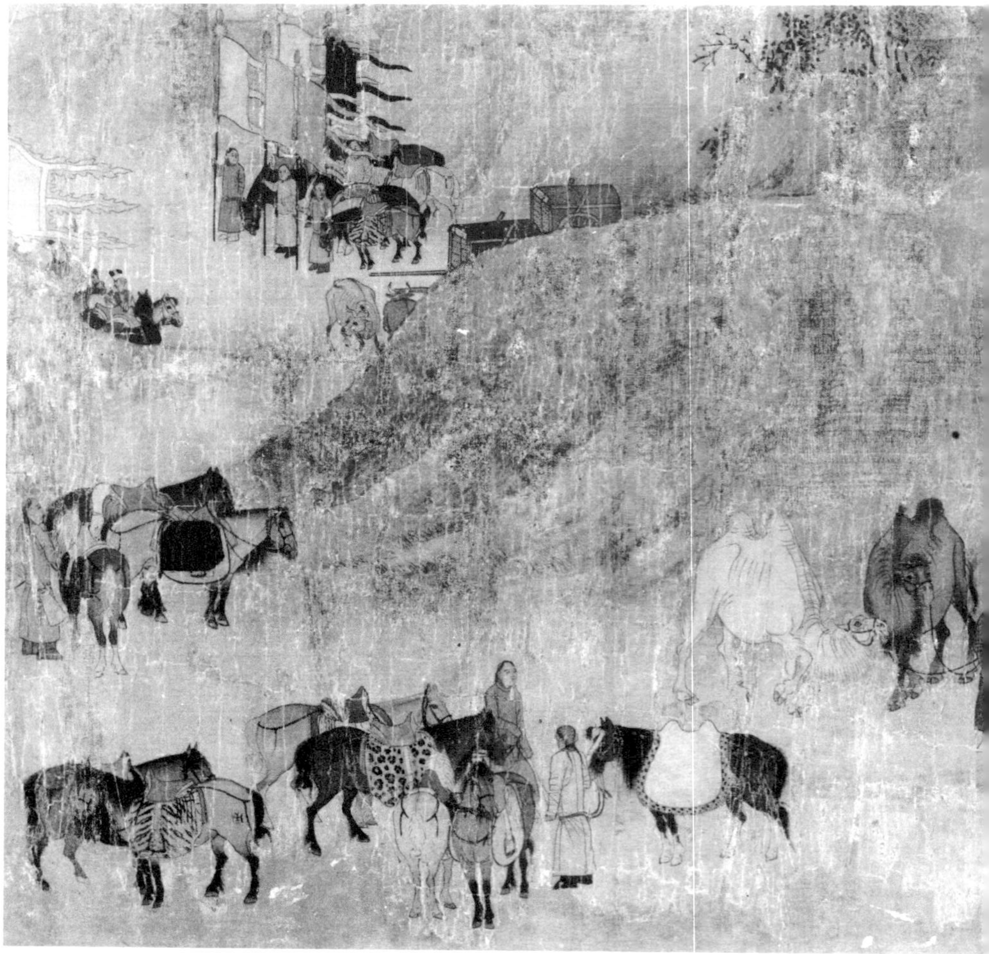

Painting for the thirteenth poem.
The Museum of Fine Arts, Boston

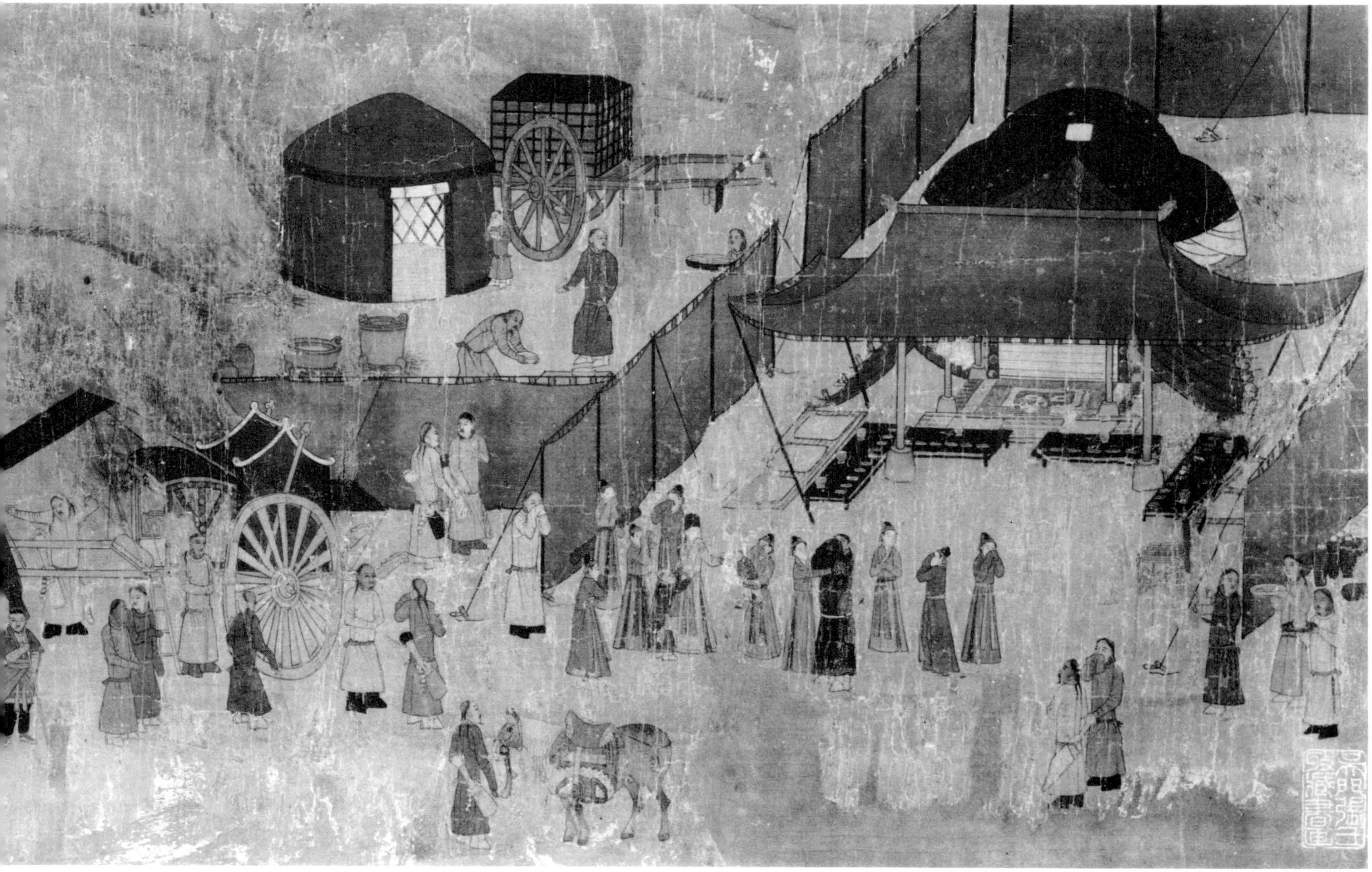

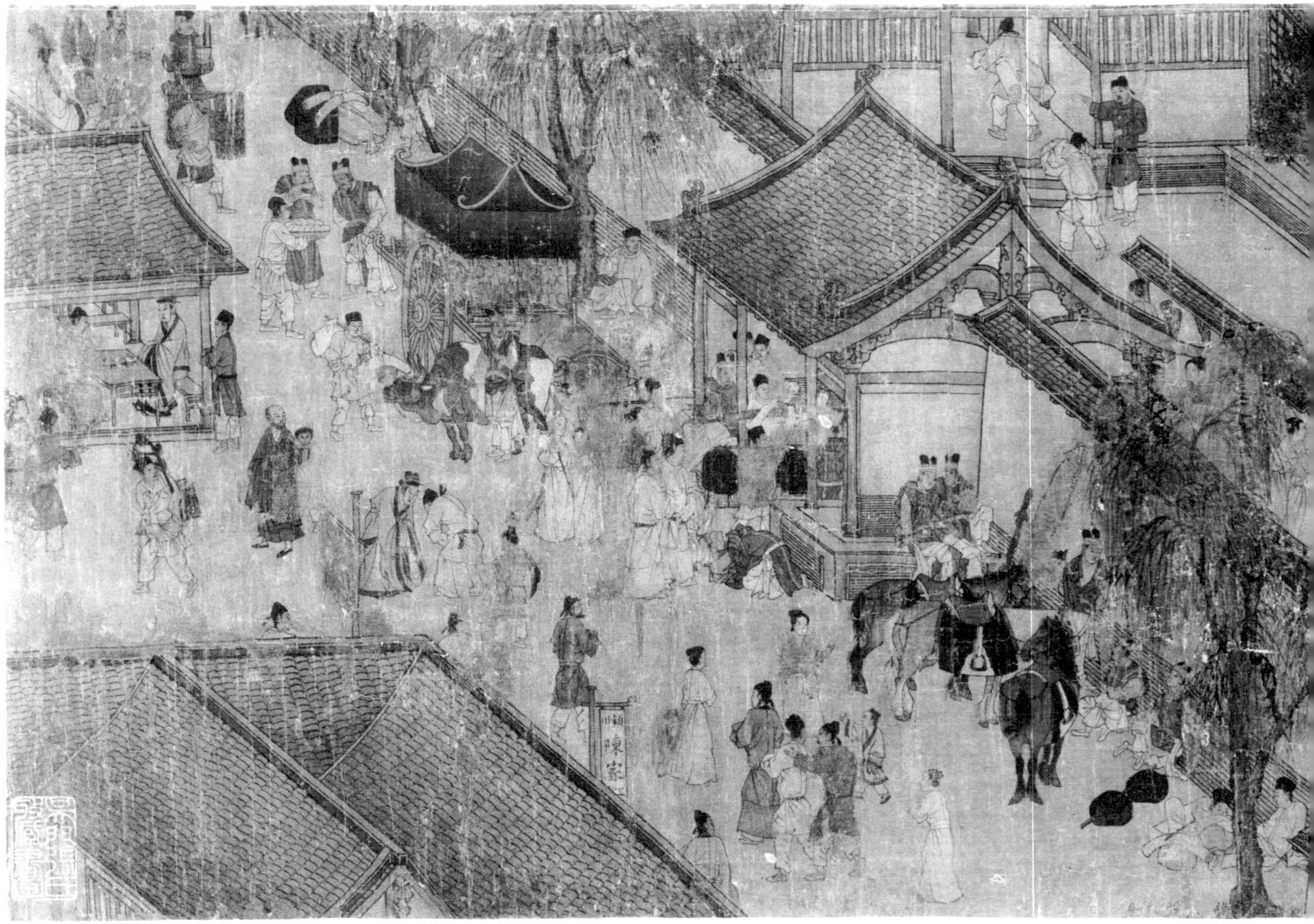

Painting for the eighteenth poem.
The Museum of Fine Arts, Boston

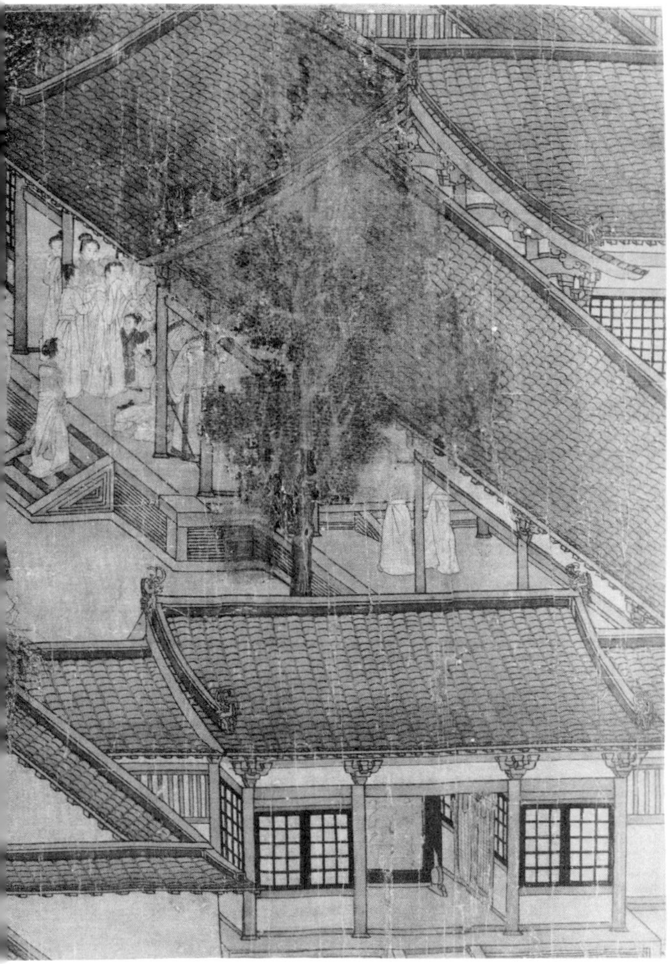

Liu Shang's poems, which survives as the four Boston pictures without texts, was created at Kao-tsung's court; a late thirteenth-century document mentions an *Eighteen Songs* with the poems in Kao-tsung's hand.[6] After he re-established the Sung state in southern China, following the overthrow of the Northern Sung by the Chin Tartars in 1126, Kao-tsung became a great art patron. Recent researches suggest that he consciously supported a program of narrative handscrolls illustrating subjects from either the classics or ancient or contemporary history as part of his governmental policy of "dynastic revival." We can readily understand the meaning the story of Wen-chi must have had for Kao-tsung, for he personally suffered grievously at the hands of the Chin Tartars: he was twice in 1126 sent to them as a hostage, and his wives, along with his father and brother, the emperors Hui-tsung and Ch'in-tsung, were captives of the Chin, and all died unransomed. An anonymous narrative handscroll of the period has recently been identified as illustrating the return from the Chin territory in 1142 of Kao-tsung's mother, the empress dowager Wei.[7] This event occurred only after years of negotiations between the Southern Sung emissaries and the Chin, and the thousand-year-old story of Lady Wen-chi must have seemed a prefiguration of the contemporary home-coming.

The Sung artist of the Boston fragments is unknown. Presumably he was a member of the emperor's Painting Academy. Clearly he was both a first-rate artist and a sensitive reporter of details of nomad life. The historical Lady Wen-chi was, as mentioned, a captive of the Southern Hsiung-nu, a Turkic tribe that plagued the Han. During the T'ang period, the Chinese knew other foes, and the nomads the poet Liu Shang had in mind, though they may have followed a similar way of life, were not the same as those who carried off the Han scholar's daughter. When the Sung painter, some three and a half centuries after Liu Shang, undertook to illustrate the T'ang retelling of the Han story, he employed imagery of his own time. While both the architecture and costumes of the Chinese portions of the scroll accurately reflect early twelfth-century Chinese life, the nomad details have been identified as those of the Liao Khitan (or Ch'i-tan), a pre-Mongol people who flourished in Manchuria and the northernmost part of China during the tenth and eleventh centuries.[8] The camel cart in the third of the Boston paintings has been compared to a similar representation in stone relief found in a Liao tomb in modern Liaoning to suggest that the Hsiung-nu of these paintings are in reality eleventh-century Khitan.[9] Wall paintings in the Ch'ing-ling mausoleum of the Liao emperors offer further proof that the nomads in the Boston paintings wear Khitan costumes and use Khitan hair styles.[10] In 1959, passages from the *History of Liao*, compiled about 1345, were cited as documentary evidence for the Khitan origin of the nomad features and costumes seen in the illustrations of the *Eighteen Songs*.[11] More recently, many of the vessels represented in the Boston paintings have been identified as Liao vessels.[12] The fact that the nomad details in the scroll paintings are Liao Khitan rather than Chin Tartar suggests that the artist received his training in the Northern Sung emperor Hui-tsung's Hsüan-ho Painting Academy, where there was a tradition of painting *fan-tsu*, "barbarian tribes."

Withal, the illustrator of the *Eighteen Songs* was a man of the Sung, and his visions and understandings of life in the northern steppes, rich though they are in exotic details, are clearly those of a Chinese.

Art-historically, it is well known that after the T'ang period the leading painters of China turned their attention from figural representation to landscape. Mi Fu (1051–1107), the scholar-artist-critic par excellence of the late Northern Sung, said flatly, "People nowadays no longer make narrative paintings."[13] In our own time it has been said that, "while the Chinese developed the landscape scroll to great height, the Japanese largely ignored landscape and developed the narrative-figural scrolls to a level hardly reached by surviving Chinese examples."[14] Be that as it may, early twelfth-century China, thanks at least in part to Kao-tsung's interest, did produce a number of narrative scrolls that matched the great Japanese narrative achievements of the late twelfth and thirteenth centuries. While those illustrating classical themes, such as Li T'ang's *Marquis Wen-kung of Chin Recovering His State* and Ma Ho-chih's *Illustrations of the Odes*,[15] show large-figured compositions firmly rooted in earlier traditions, scrolls such as the *Eighteen Songs* and Chang Tse-tuan's *Ch'ing-ming Festival on the River*[16] display a mastery of realism and passion for drama unparalleled in the history of Chinese art.

Recounting a historical drama in contemporary details, the pictures of the *Eighteen Songs* translate Liu Shang's poems into vivid images. We see it all: the contrast between the comforts and embellishments of Chinese city life and the bleak existence in the steppes; the emphasis on what were, for the Chinese, the nomads' revolting personal habits; the desperate loneliness of a captive nearly cut off from human communication by the language barrier; and finally, the deep hatred for an enemy turning unexpectedly into an even deeper love for a spouse and children. In the decades following the Sung dynasty's retreat to southern China, similar stories of severed ties and reunions must have been the lot of numberless northern Chinese families escaped to the south. When we recall the years of bitter political intrigues and quarrels that revolved around Kao-tsung's halfhearted efforts at ransoming the emperors Hui and Ch'in, and how these quarrels ended only with the return in 1142 of the empress dowager Wei, bringing with her the mortal remains of the unfortunate older emperors, it may fairly be said that to the early Southern Sung viewer the *Eighteen Songs* represented no mere historical romance but a real, all-pervading national trauma.

NOTES

1. Wen Fong, *Sung and Yuan Paintings* (The Metropolitan Museum of Art, 1973), pages 36–40, 139–140.

2. The story is found in the *Hou Han-shu* (*History of the Latter Han Dynasty*) (1739 edition), *chüan* 114, pages 16a–19a. See also Kojiro Tomita, "Wen-chi's Captivity in Mongolia and Her Return to China," *Museum of Fine Arts Bulletin* (Boston, 1928), Vol. 26, pages 40–45; John F. Haskins, "The Pazyryk Felt Screen and the Barbarian Captivity of Ts'ai Wen Chi," *Museum of Far Eastern Antiquities Bulletin* (Stockholm, 1963), No. 35, pages 141–161; *Hu-chia shih-pa-p'ai t'ao-lun chi* (*A Collection of Essays on "The Eighteen Songs of a Nomad Flute"*) (Peking, 1959).

3. The *Hu-chia shih-pa-p'ai* (*Eighteen Songs of a Nomad Flute*) attributed to Wen-chi are found in the *Ch'u-tz'u hou-yü*, edited by Chu Hsi (1130–1200), *chüan* 3, pages 12b–19b. Despite the "flute" in the title, the songs were meant to be accompanied by the stringed *ch'in*.

4. See *Ch'üan T'ang-shih* (*chüan* 303) (Peking, 1960), Vol. 5, pages 3450–53.

5. There are six important versions of the *Eighteen Songs* illustrations:
   1. The album leaves in the Museum of Fine Arts, Boston (the original).
   2. The handscroll in The Metropolitan Museum of Art, accession number 1973.120.3.
   3. Eighteen paintings reproduced in the periodical *I-lin yüeh-k'an* (Peking, 1930–34).
   4. An album of eighteen paintings entitled *Wen-chi kuei Han t'u*, National Palace Museum, Taiwan, described in *Ku-kung shu-hua-lu* (Taipei, 1956), Vol. VI, pages 4–9.
   5. A handscroll with eighteen illustrations, Yamato Bunkakan, Nara, Japan; see Shujiro Shimada, "Concerning the Handscroll Painting of Wen-chi's Return to China" (in Japanese), *Yamato bunka* (Nara, 1962), No. 37, pages 18–30.
   6. A handscroll with eighteen illustrations, Nanking Museum; see *Hu-chia shih-pa-p'ai* (Shanghai, 1961).

   Numbers 2, 4, and 5 present the illustrations and texts of Liu Shang's poems in precisely the same order. A street sign in the fourth leaf of Number 1 identifies the city as Ying-ch'üan, or Ch'en-liu. The sign is blank in both the Ch'en-liu scenes in the Metropolitan Museum's scroll, but the inscription is present in the first scene of Number 5, suggesting that Number 5, a late Ming copy, is unrelated, as a copy, to Number 2. Number 6, another late Ming copy, shows a makeshift attempt to fit the illustrations to the poems attributed to Wen-chi, rather than to the cycle of Liu Shang, with the result that scenes five, six, eight, and nine of the original scroll appear as scenes six, five, nine, and eight.

6. Chuang Su, *Hua-chi pu-i* (1298), reprint edited by Huang Miao-tzu (Peking, 1963), page 8. For discussion of Kao-tsung's role, see Fong, *Sung and Yuan Paintings*, pages 29–43.

7. Hsü Pang-ta, "A Study on the Identification of a Narrative Painting as *Welcoming the Imperial Carriages*" (in Chinese), *Wen-wu* (Peking, 1972), No. 8, pages 61–63. The scroll is reproduced (four illustrations) in *T'ang Sung Yüan Ming Ch'ing hua-hsüan* (*Selected Paintings of the T'ang, Sung, Yüan, Ming, and Ch'ing Dynasties*) (Canton, 1963), No. 12.

8. Karl A. Wittfogel and Feng Chia-sheng, *History of Chinese Society: Liao (907–1125)* (New York, 1949), especially page 21 and following.

9. Ryuzo Torii, *Sculptured Stone Tombs of the Liao Dynasty* (Harvard–Yenching Institute, 1942), pages 70–72, 74–85.

10. Jitsuzo Tamura and Yukio Kobayashi, *Tombs and Mural Paintings of Ch'ing-ling* (Kyoto, 1953), Vol. II, plates 20 and following.

11. Wang Ch'ü-fei, "Concerning Some Problems about a Ming Copy of 'The Eighteen Songs of a Nomad Flute'" (in Chinese), *Wen-wu* (1959), No. 6, pages 35–37.

12. Jan Fontein and Tung Wu, *Unearthing China's Past* (Museum of Fine Arts, Boston, 1973), pages 221–224. And Dr. Fontein has called our attention to recent archaeological reports on a newly discovered Liao dynasty tomb at Kulun Banner, in which wall paintings, depicting Liao nobility departing on and returning from a trip, give further pictorial evidence of Liao costumes and accouterments, including the gathered drums and the camel cart; see Wang Tse-ch'ing, "A Tentative Interpretation of the Wall Painting of the Liao Tomb Number 1 at Kulun Banner, Kirin Province" (in Chinese), *Wen-wu* (1973), No. 8, pages 30–35.

13. *Hua-shih*, in *Mei-shu ts'ung-shu* edition (Shanghai, 1947), II, 9/1, page 8b.

14. Sherman E. Lee, *A History of Far Eastern Art* (New York, 1964), page 328.

15. Fong, *Sung and Yuan Paintings*, pages 29–36, 41–51.

16. Reproduced as *Sung Chang Tse-tuan Ch'ing-ming shang-ho-t'u chüan* (*The Ch'ing-ming Festival on the River by Chang Tse-tuan*) (Peking, 1958).

ADDITIONAL NOTES

The Chinese characters on the title page, extracted from the calligraphy of the eighteenth poem, read "Nomad Flute, Eighteen Songs." The eighteen poems are highly formal, with strictly controlled patterns and rhymes. Our translations, kept as literal as possible, rely on line division and punctuation to suggest the originals.

ACKNOWLEDGMENTS

Very helpful to us in the problems encountered in writing the text for this publication have been these colleagues and associates, and we thank them all warmly:

Schuyler Cammann,
University of Pennsylvania

Walter A. Fairservis, Jr., and his assistant Brian Garrison,
American Museum of Natural History

Jan Fontein,
Museum of Fine Arts, Boston

John F. Haskins,
University of Pittsburgh

Shujiro Shimada,
Princeton University

and Marilyn Fu, Jean Mailey, Helmut Nickel, and Suzanne G. Valenstein,
The Metropolitan Museum of Art

R. A. R. and W. F.

Eighteen Songs of a Nomad Flute

1 The Abduction of Wen-chi

The Han house is declining, the barbarians of the four directions have
become unfriendly;
They raise arms, and wars are incessant.
Pity my father and mother who bore and reared me:
For witnessing partings and turmoil—this is the moment.
At gauze windows, looking into mirrors, I had not experienced the
world;
I thought that the beaded curtains could shelter me.
One day the barbarian cavalry entered China;
Suddenly everywhere we met nomads.
My unfortunate life is now at sword's point,
Alas, a helpless woman carried away into the aliens' dust.

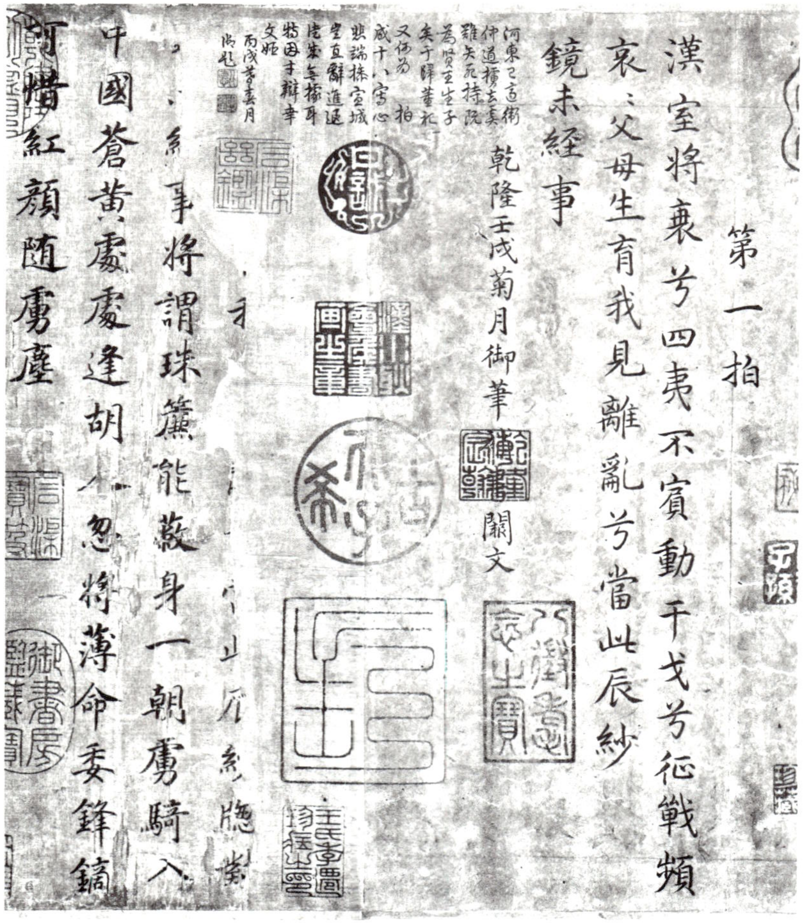

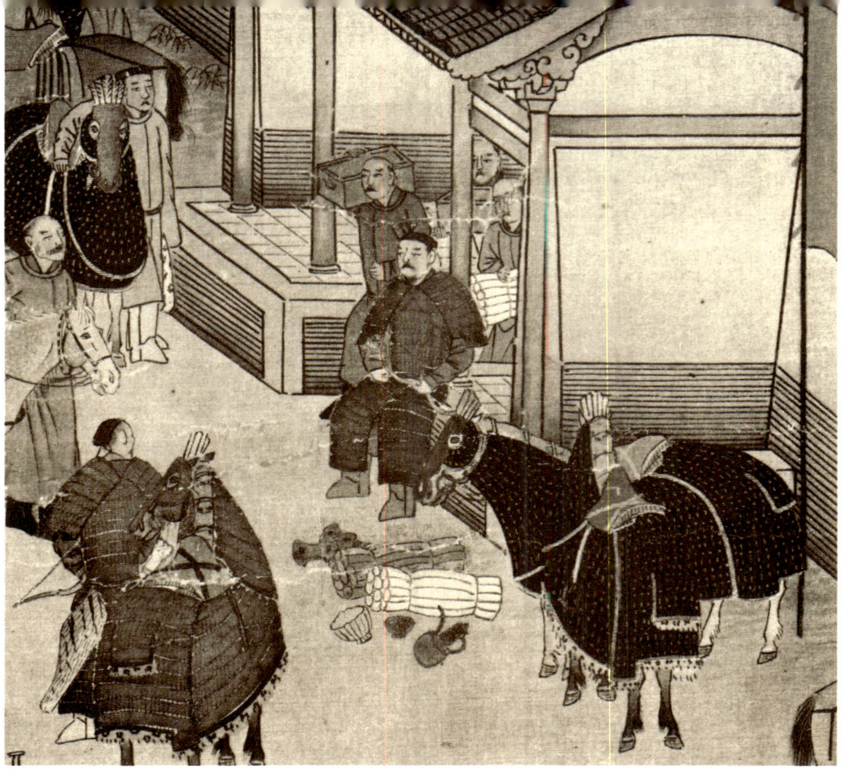

Beneath the invaders' banners loom the frightening forms of armored men and horses. Blood has been spilled: defenseless people of the city hurry past a body. In a moment there will be another casualty: a servant, scrambling over a wall, is about to receive an arrow. Another, fleeing along a loggia, will not escape his pursuer. At the entrance to Ts'ai Yung's compound a captain sits at ease while loot from within is added to the pile before him. In the courtyard, clad in his gilded armor, the band's chief examines the prize being presented to him: the daughter of the house.

A street sign in the fourth of the Boston paintings (it is blank here) identifies this scene as Ying-ch'üan, or Ch'en-liu. The compound, with its spacious courtyards and open loggias, is a good example of an elegant early Southern Sung residence in the Chiang-nan area.

The nomad (actually Khitan) soldiers have shaved heads with queues hanging at the sides. The officers wear soft caps. The horses are clad in armor of leather and iron. In the 1130s the Southern Sung army was threatened by the *kuai-tzu-ma* of the Chin general Wu-chu: a cavalry force with these armored horses chained together in threes. It is said that the Sung general Yüeh Fei destroyed such a military machine by ordering foot soldiers with sickles to go under the charging force and chop down the horses' unprotected legs.

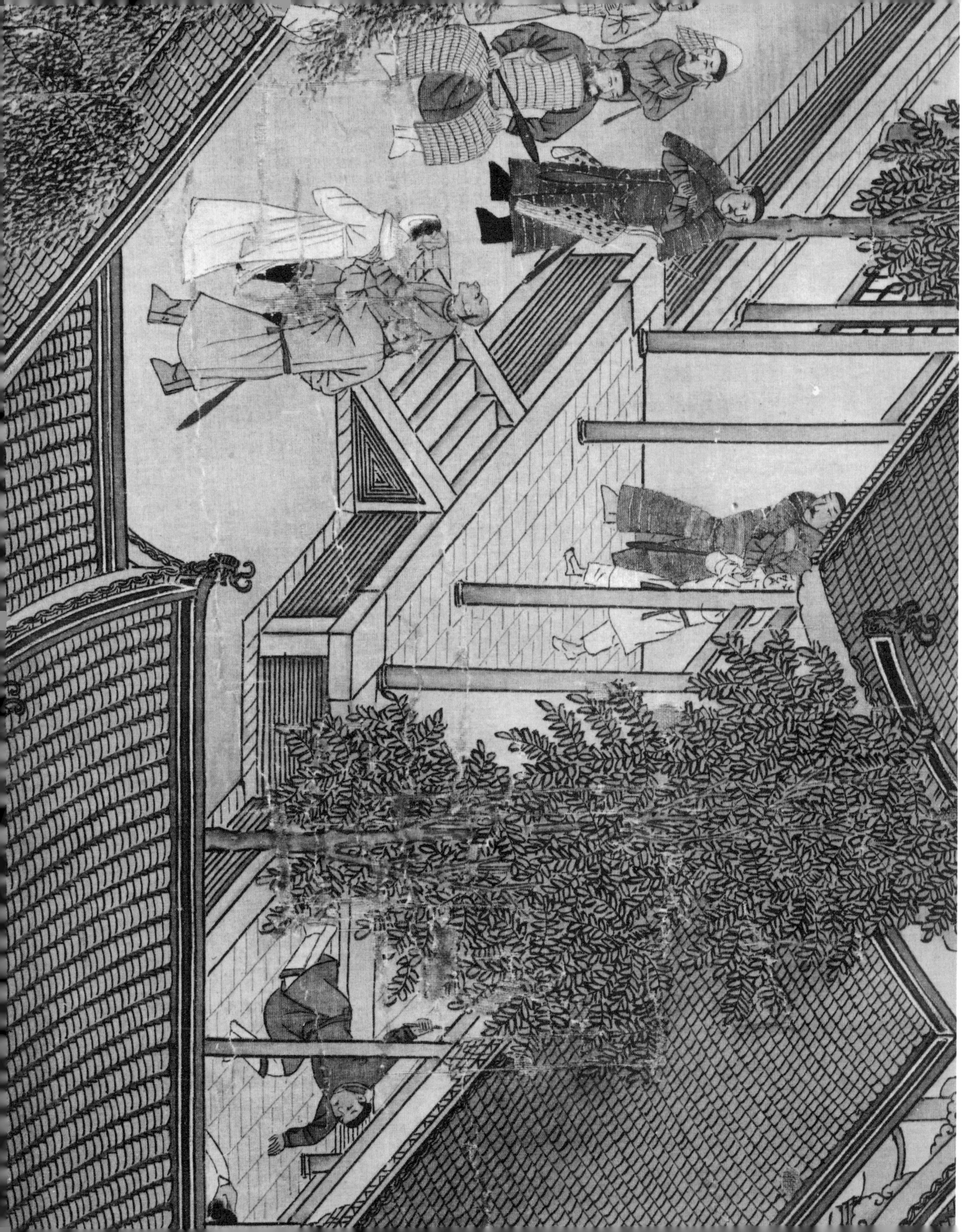

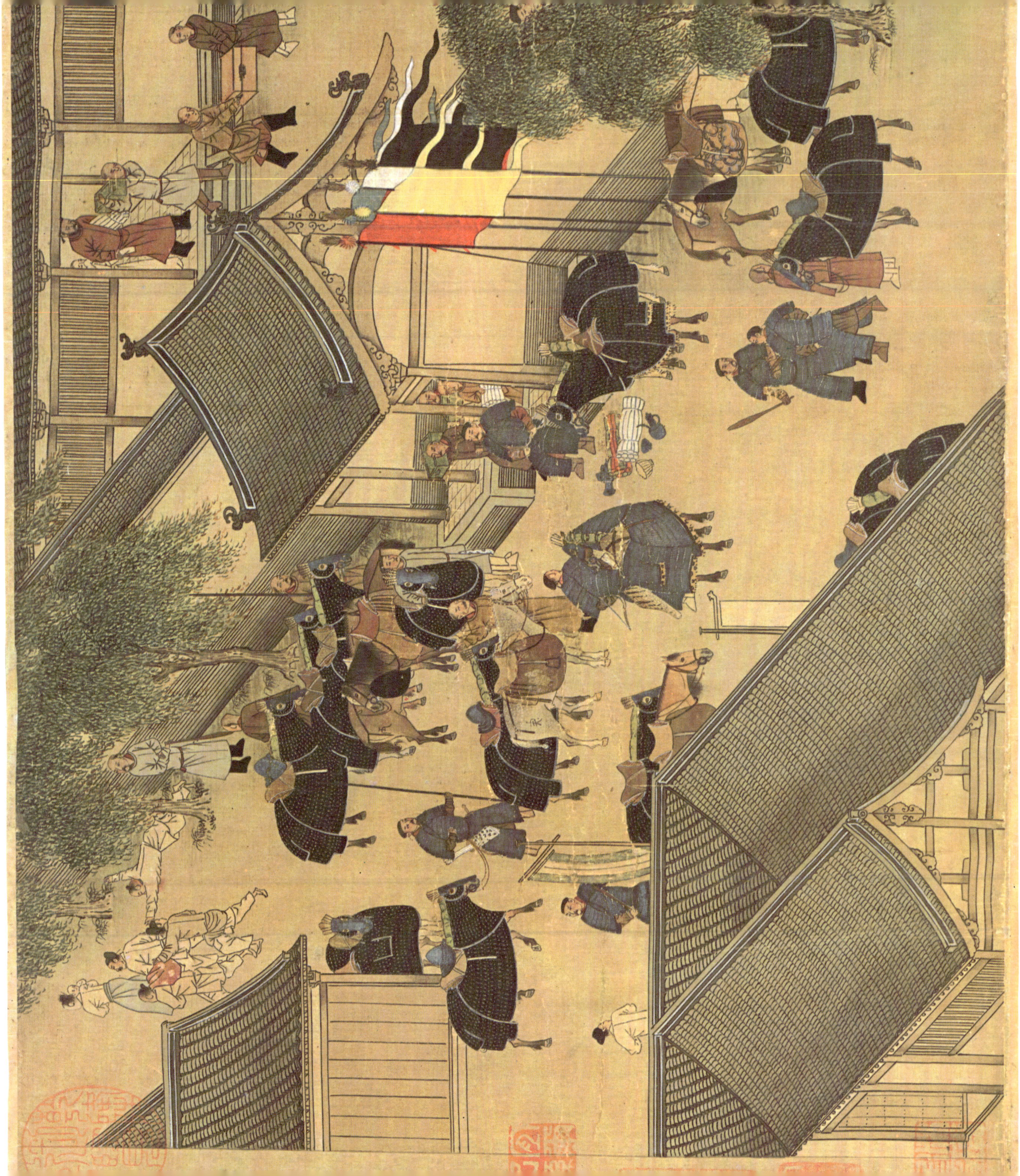

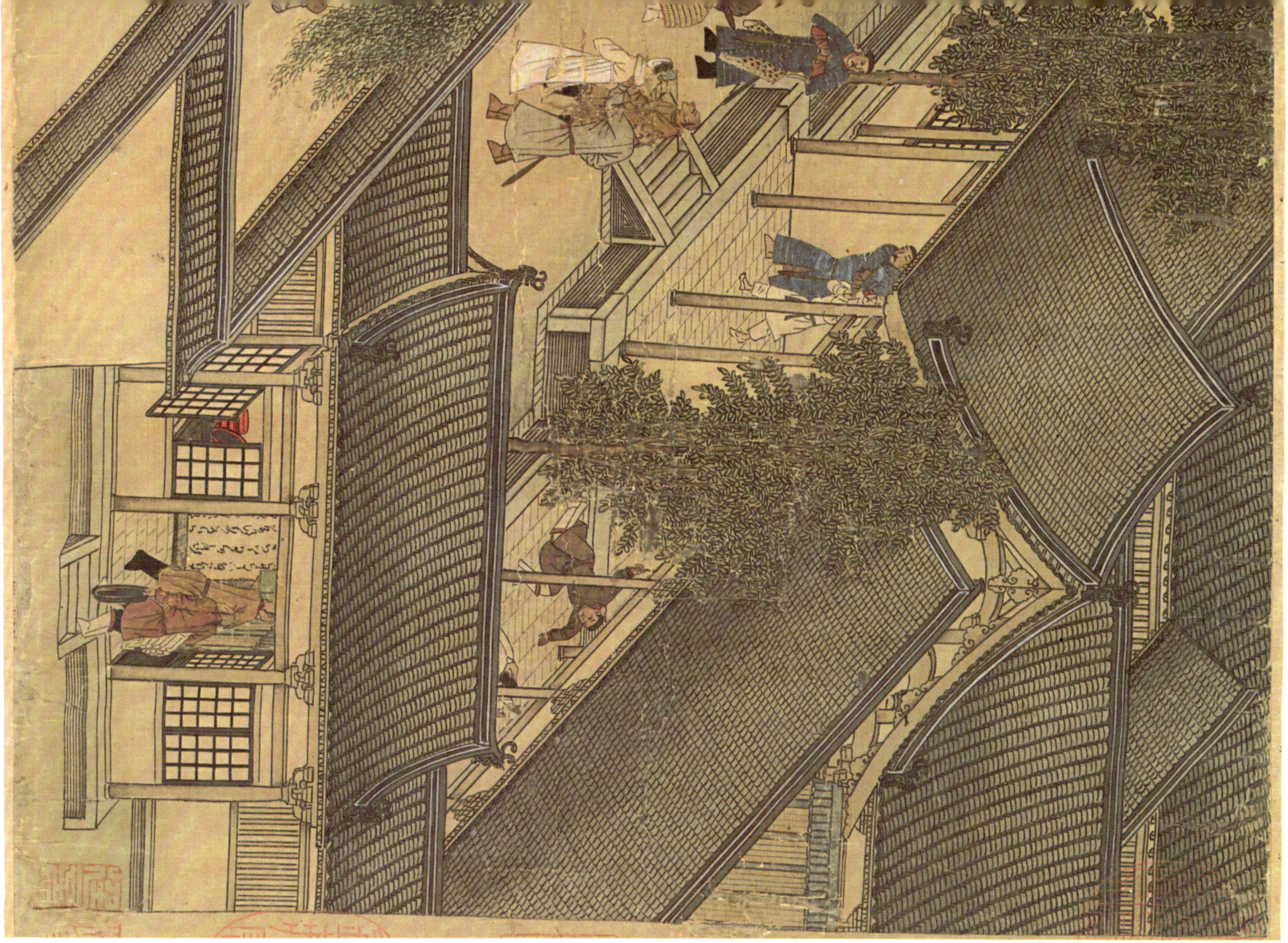

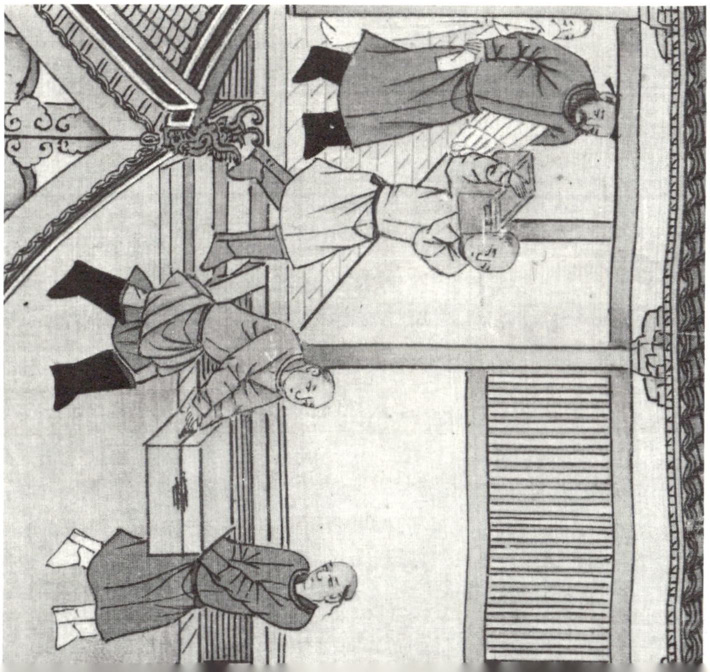

2 Departure from China

I was taken on horseback to the ends of the earth;
Tiring of life, I sought death, but death would not come.
The barbarians stink so. How can they be considered human?
Their pleasures and angers are like the jackal's and the wolf's—how unbearable!
We travel to the end of Tien-shan, enduring all the frost and sleet;*
The customs are rude, the land is desolate—we are near the nomads' territories.
An overcast sky stretches beyond ten thousand miles. Not a single bird is in sight.
The cold sands are boundless: one can no longer tell the south from the north.

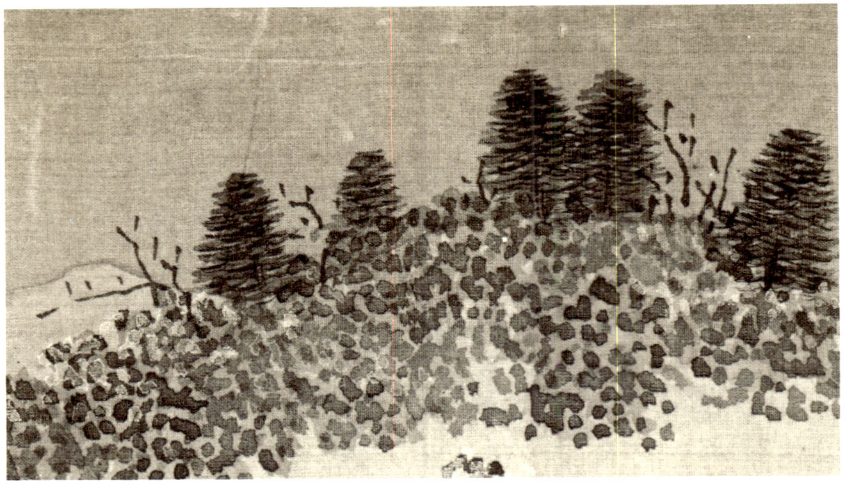

*Mountains in the far west, in modern Sinkiang province. This is figurative speech; Wen-chi's party did not go that far west.

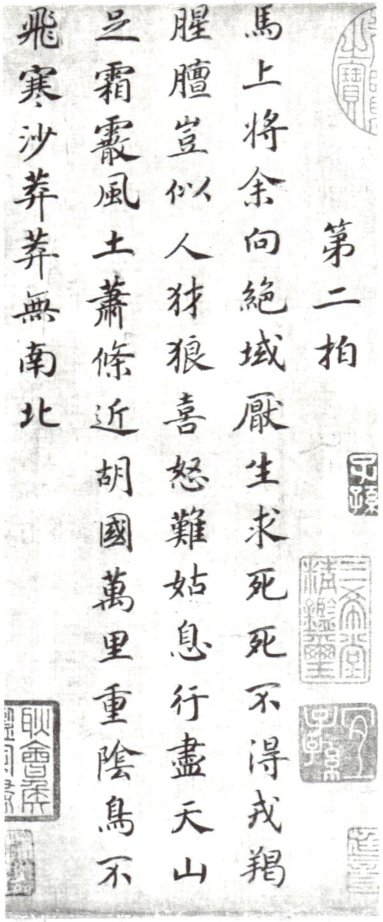

第二拍
馬上將余向絕域厭生求死死不得戎羯
腥膻豈似人豺狼喜怒難姑息行盡天山
足霜霰風土蕭條近胡國萬里重陰鳥不
飛寒沙莽莽無南北

Wearing an ermine-trimmed hat and riding a white-footed horse with a blaze, the nomad leader watches his captive. Wen-chi has been given a dappled horse with snow-leopard saddle skin, and she wears a traveling hat with veil. The tribal banners show the cardinal directions (a symbolism borrowed from China): red—south, green—east, white—west, black—north, yellow—center. Flute music is heard above the beating of hooves. The chieftain's remount, its saddle decorated with plumes, follows the banners. The chieftain's falconer rides with a bird on his gloved arm. Through the trees one glimpses horses laden with baggage and plunder. The armor, no longer needed, has been packed away, but the tails of the ponies are still knotted short, campaign-style.

Sparse vegetation, growing mostly on one side of the hills, tells us we are far north of the land Wen-chi knew as home. The round foliage dots derive from the tradition of the great Northern Sung landscapist Fan K'uan (about 1000). A snowscape by Liang K'ai (about 1200) showing two nomad horsemen at the foot of a mountain also has the Fan K'uan-inspired foliage dots (*Sogen no meiga* [Tokyo National Museum, 1962], plate 100). It is possible that Liang K'ai, who in his earlier career was an Academy painter, derived his inspiration from a representation of the Wen-chi story. A hat like Wen-chi's is worn by a woman in Chao Kan's late tenth-century painting *Early Snow on the River* (*Three Hundred Masterpieces of Chinese Painting in the Palace Museum* [Taipei, 1959], Vol II, No. 50).

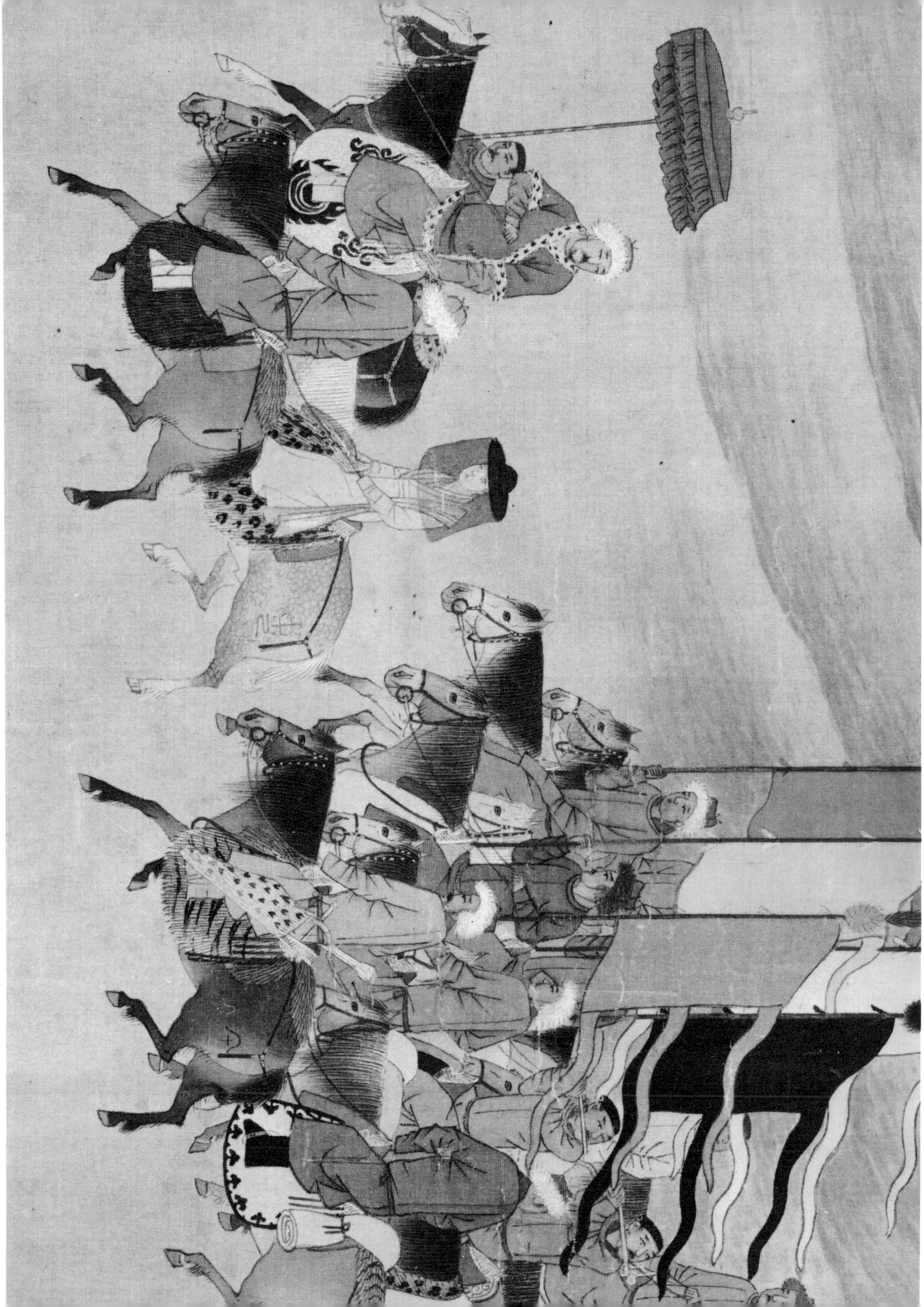

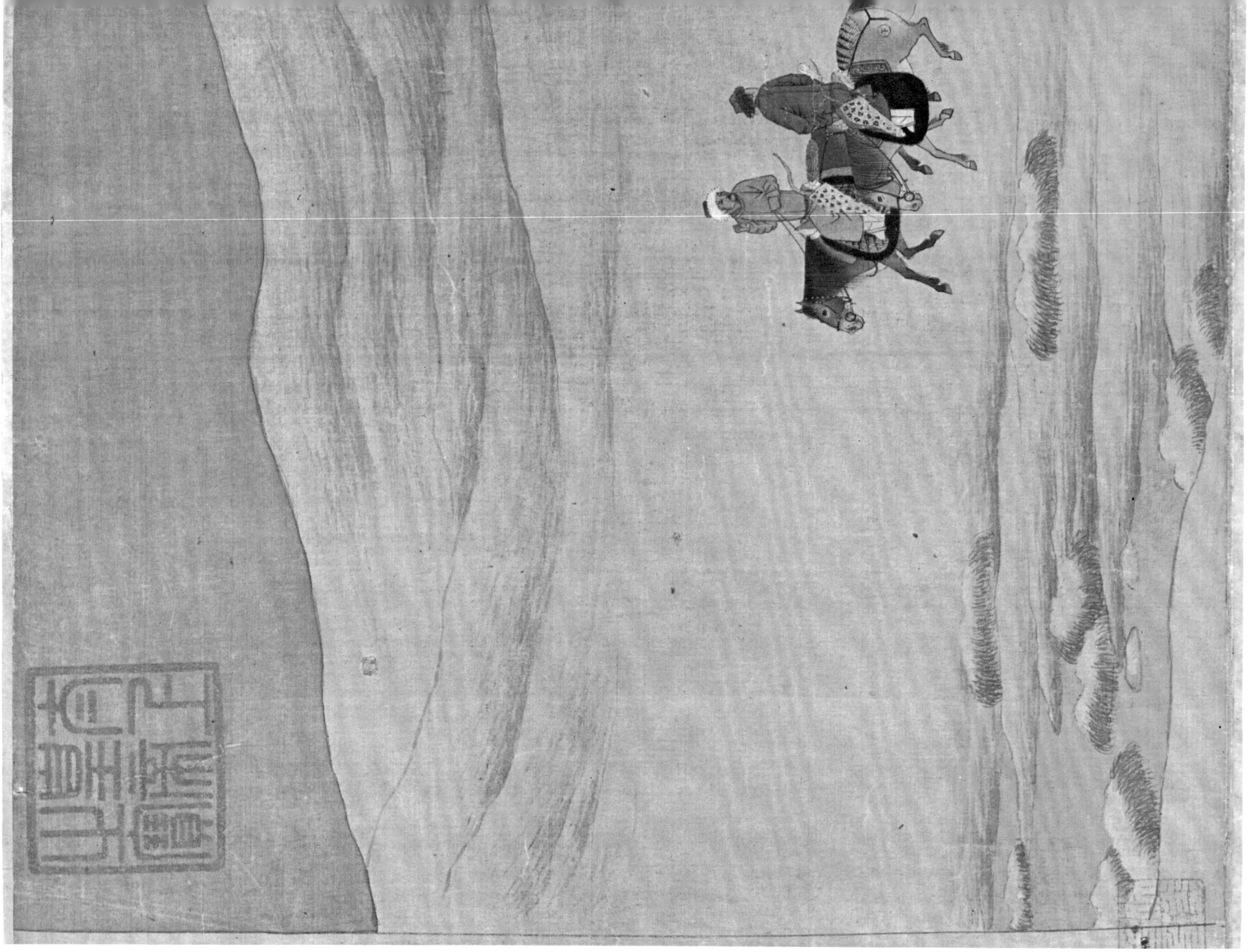

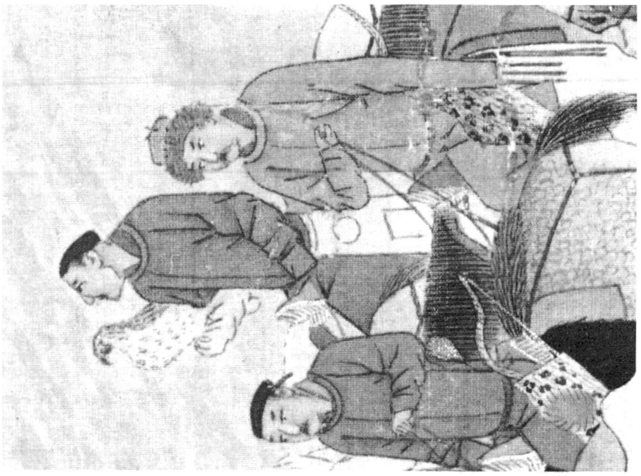

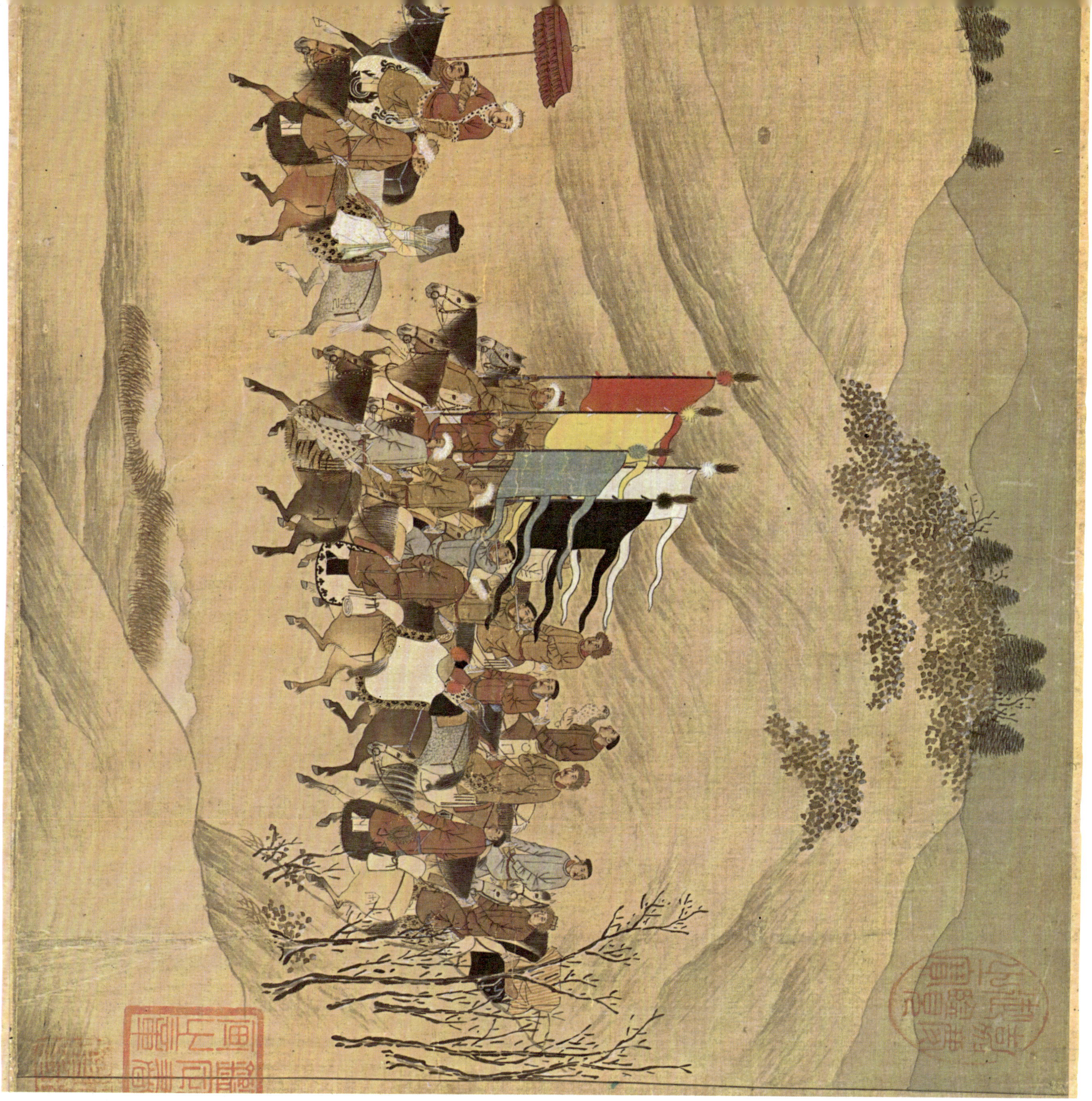

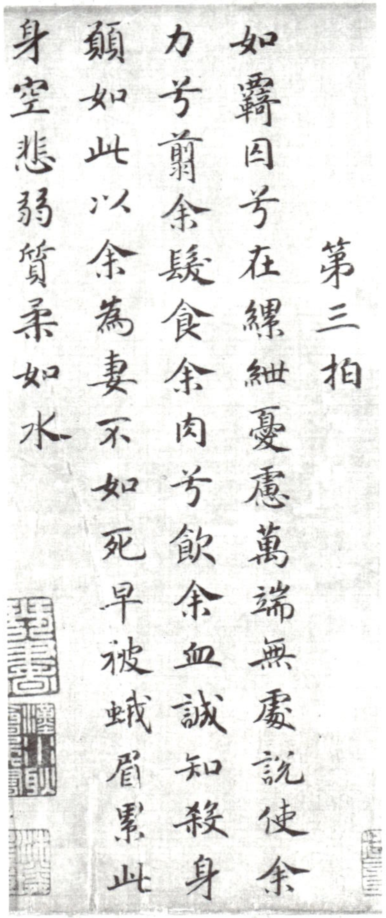

3 Encampment in the Desert

I am like a prisoner in bonds,
I have ten thousand anxieties but no one to confide them to.
They can make me work, or they can cut my hair;
They can eat my flesh, and they can drink my blood.
Knowing this is death, I would suffer anything willingly,
But to make me his wife is worse than killing me.
Alas, how a pretty face has made me suffer,
How I resent it that I am weak and soft like water.

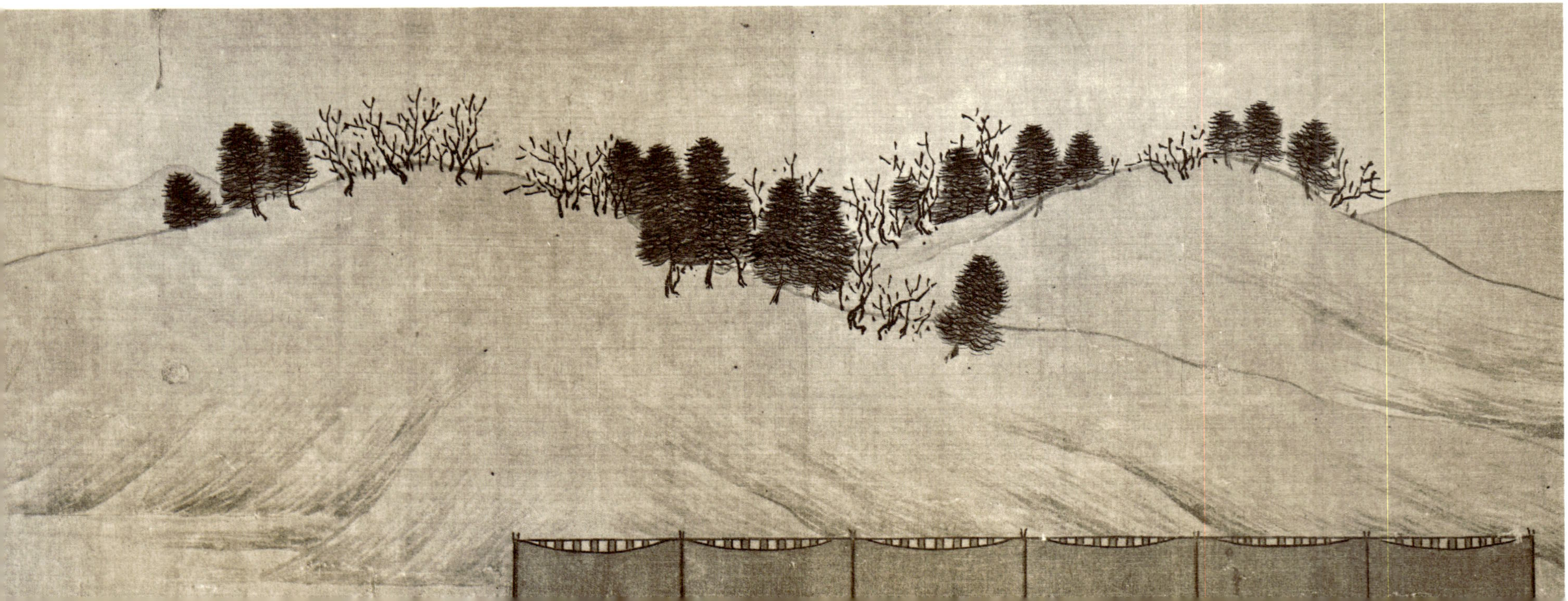

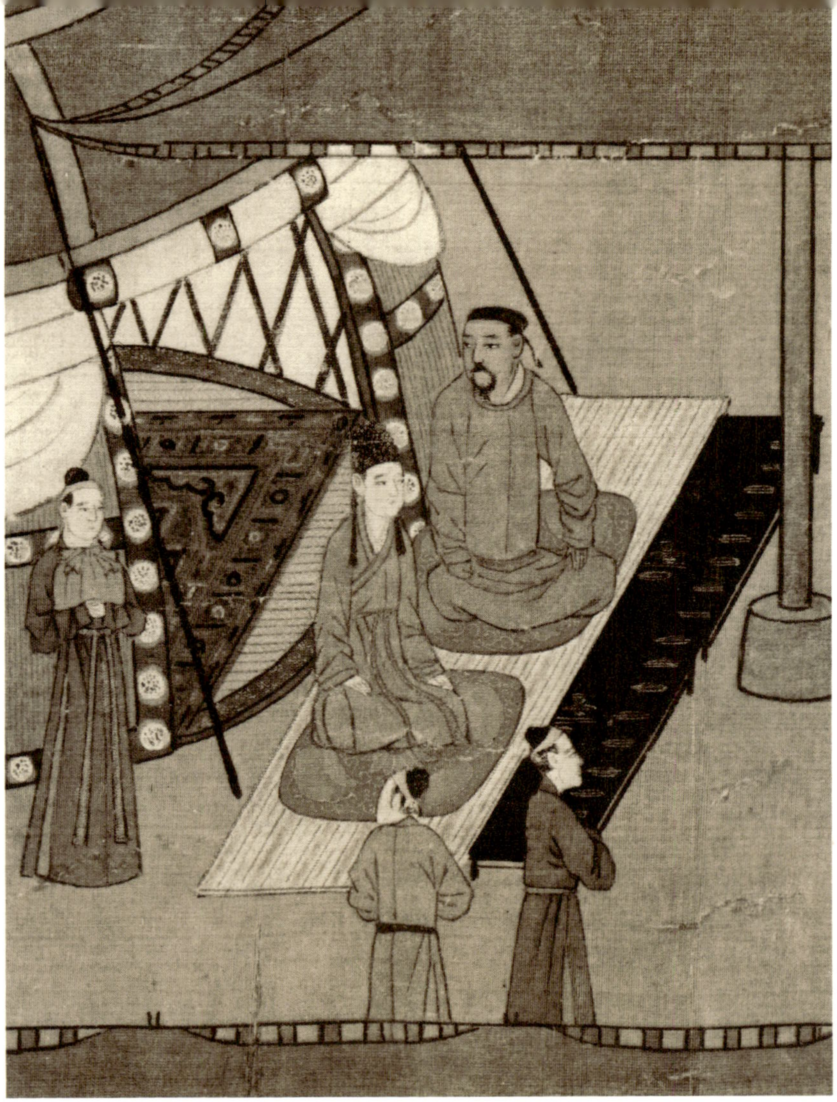

According to the *History of Liao* (about 1345), the Liao emperors, ruling northern China, dressed in Chinese style, while their empresses wore Khitan costumes (Introduction, note 11). Here the nomad chief wears the informal garb of a Chinese ruler, while Wen-chi is dressed like a Khitan princess, wearing a high, brimless black gauze hat with two long flaps hanging at the sides.

Screens of felt mounted on canes protect the chieftain's quarters from the winds blowing off the thinly wooded hills. The handsome scissor-latticed yurt is floored with matting and a pile rug. A canopy shelters the couple at their meal, which is being served by both men and women. Gold dishes are on the two low tables placed end to end. A tall red-lacquered table, conspicuously elegant in this setting, is a Chinese import. Beside the table are stoneware jars of Liao type. Wen-chi, sitting wooden-faced, is obviously not impressed with the tribe's efforts to please her, nor with her consort's gentle attentiveness.

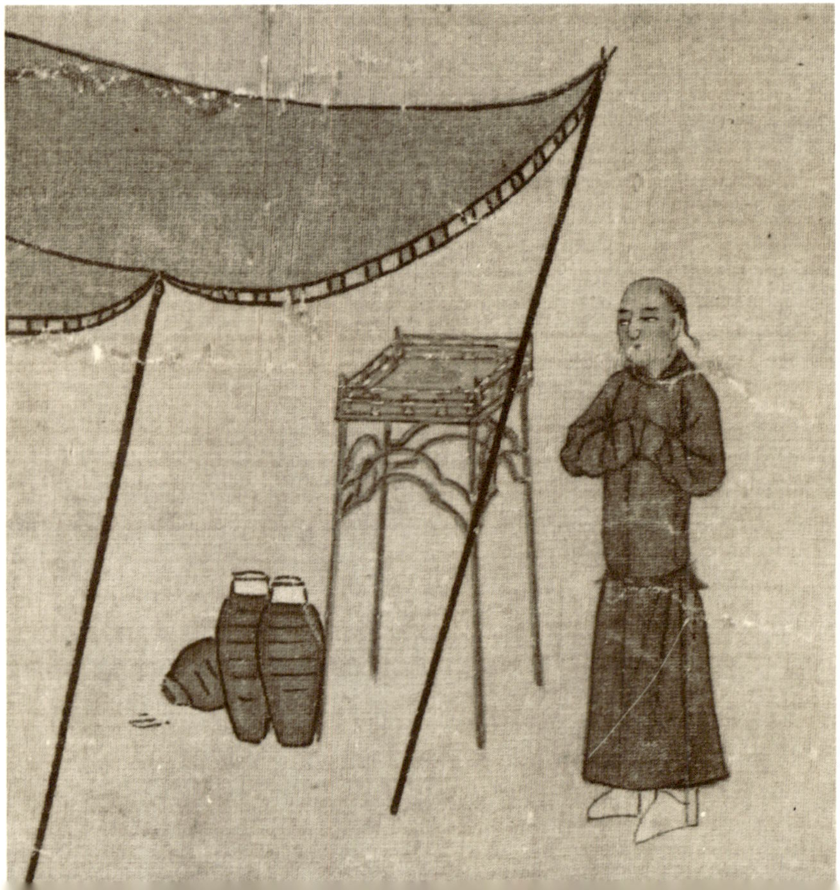

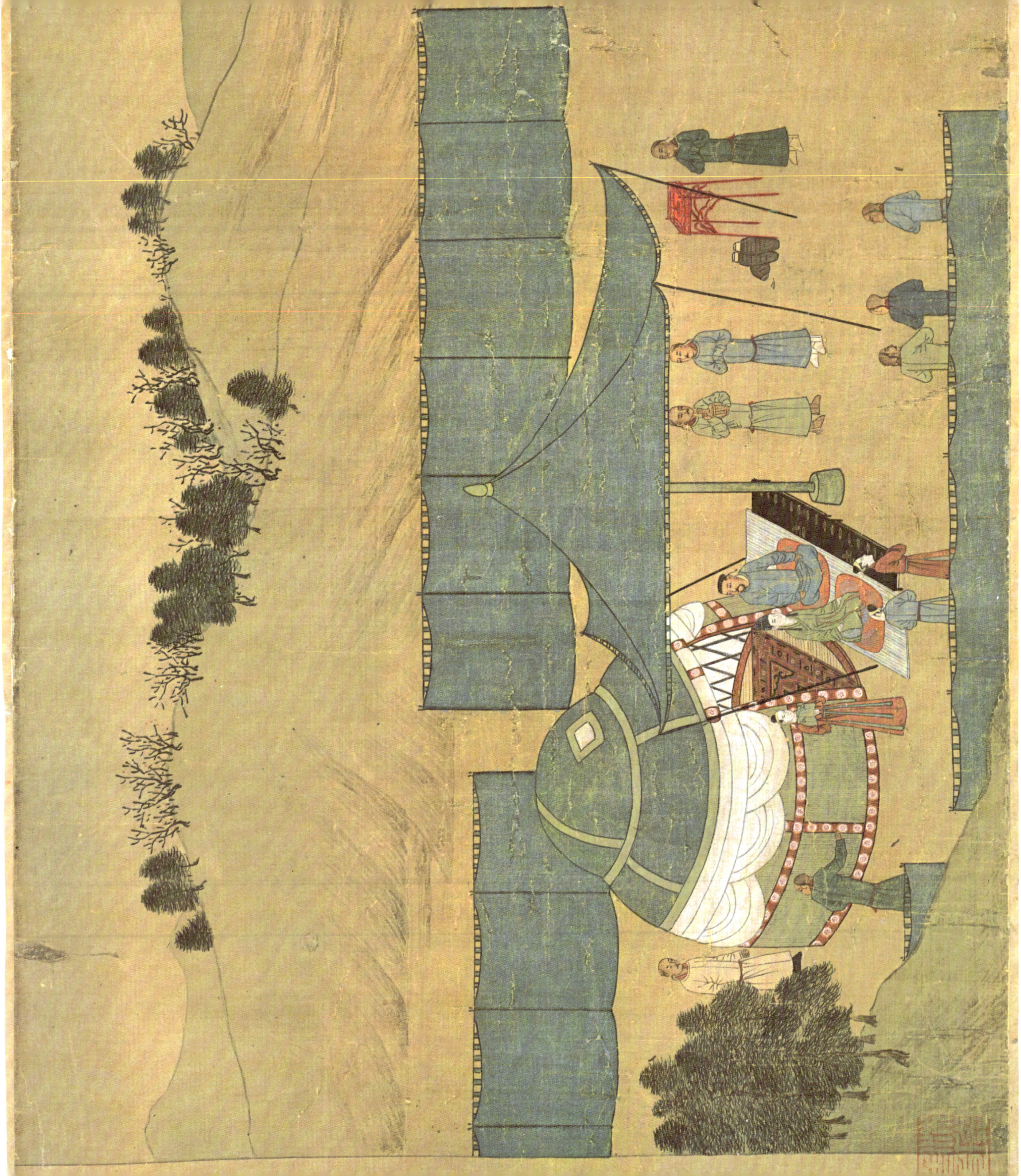

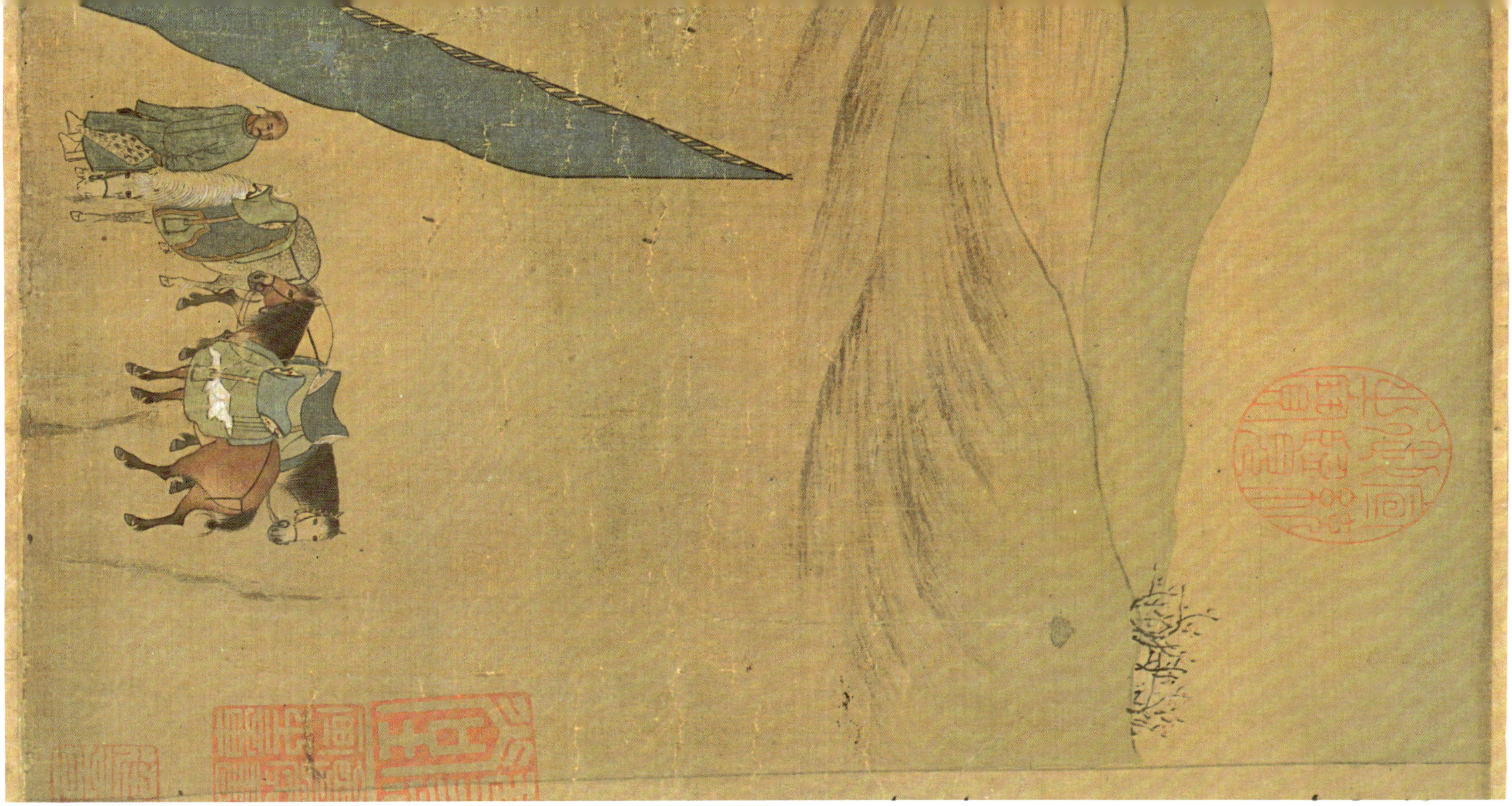

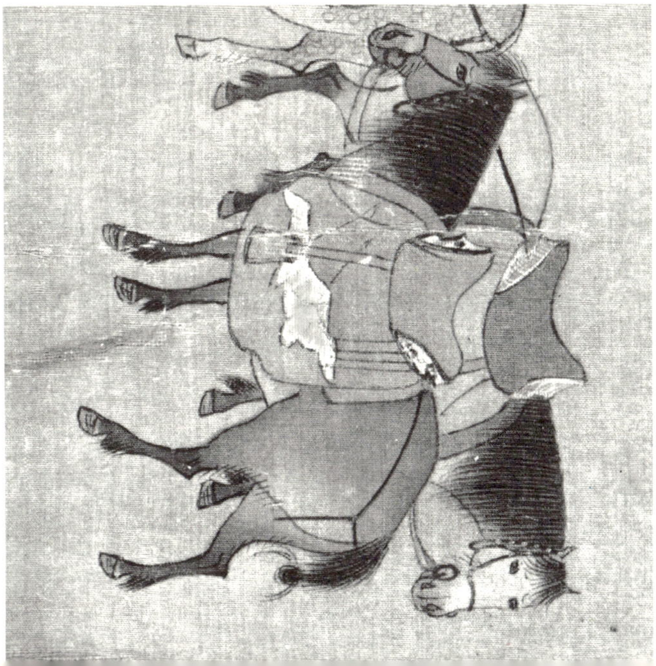

4 Longing for Home

Mountains and streams a long way away—who can remember them?
Where, at the sky's edge, is my native land?
Since my terrifying experience my energy has faded.
Gradually, wind and frost have ravaged my countenance.
In the night I dream of returning, to and fro;
In my half-dreaming state is it possible that some messages may be transmitted?
In the vast barbarian sky my cries are not answered,
Yet the bright moon is my Han moon, which should recognize me.

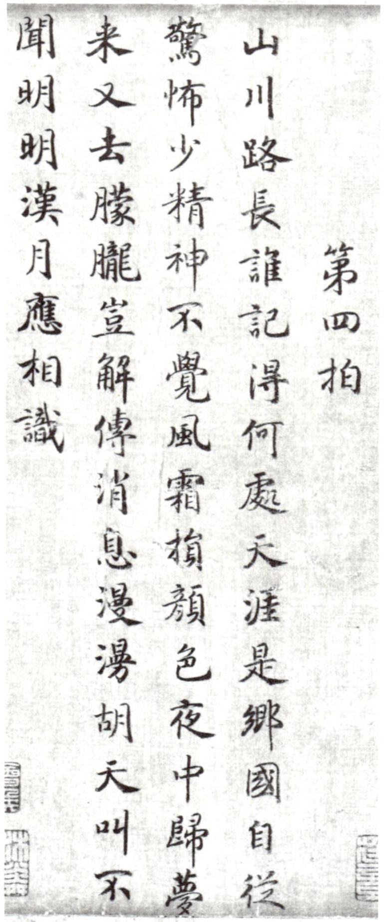

第四拍

山川路長誰記得何處天涯是鄉國自從
驚怖少精神不覺風霜損顏色夜中歸夢
来又去朦朧豈解傳消息漫漫胡天叫不
聞明明漢月應相識

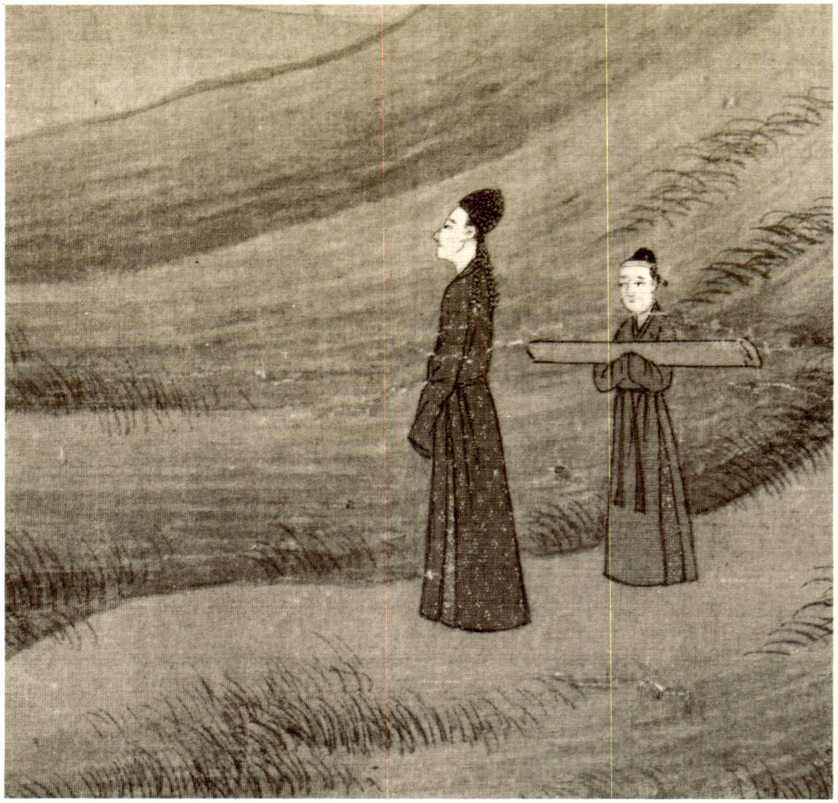

Auburn leaves declare the passing of another year. Wen-chi, her back turned upon the yurts and saddles of the camp, gazes despondently at the moon across the barren landscape. Not everything of her past is lost, for a girl attendant carries her *ch'in*, the classic Chinese stringed instrument, in its protective wrapping.

The painter here sets the mode for the related compositions of the sixth, ninth, and eleventh scenes. In the poems for these scenes the poet continues to describe Wen-chi's bereavement and loneliness; each time, the painter selects a concrete image for his illustration: the moon, the constellation of the Dipper, horsemen shooting the messenger birds, migrating geese as direction-pointers. With the slopes and campsites pushed to the right side, the viewer's attention is directed to the chosen theme in the upper left corner of the picture.

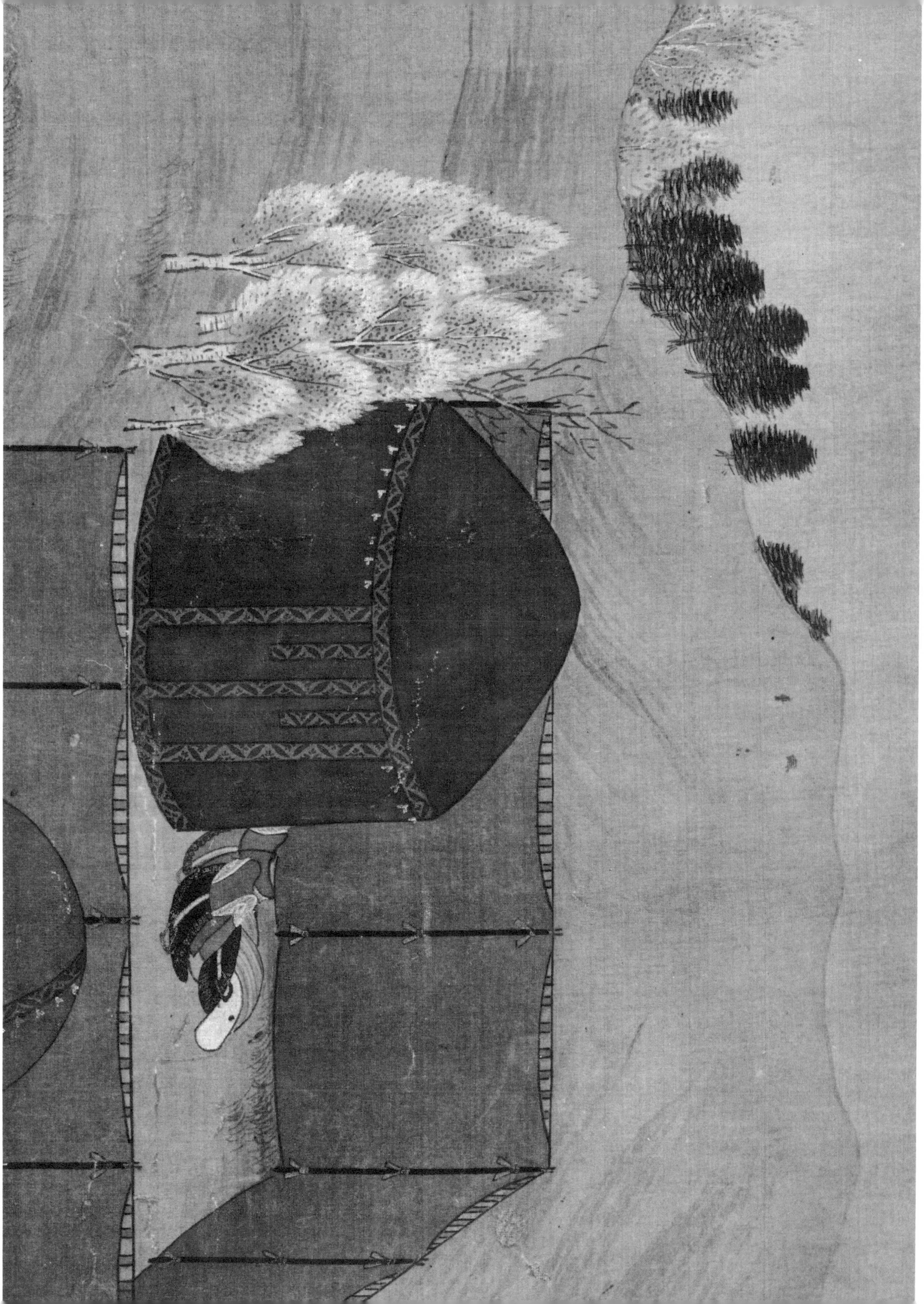

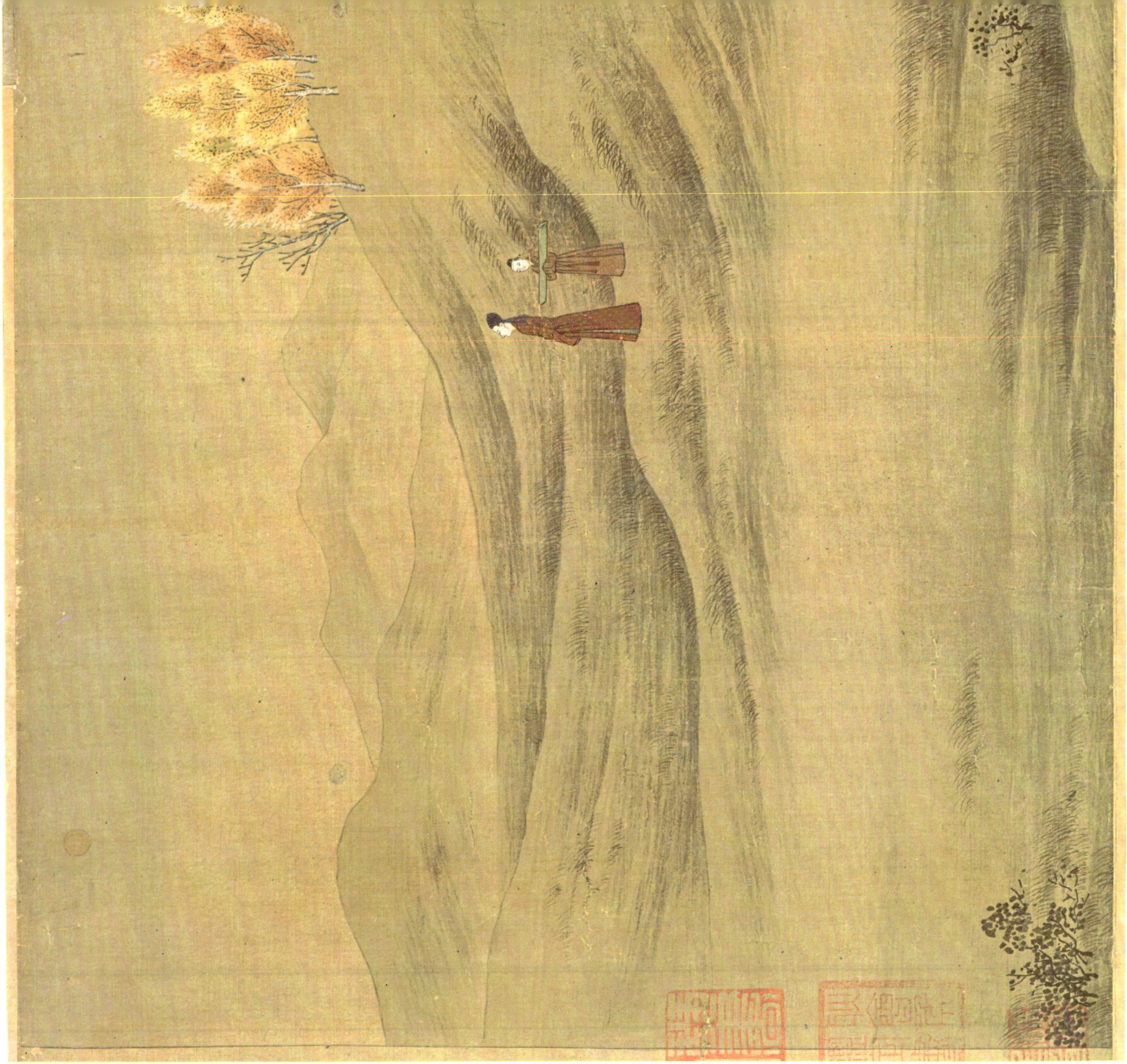

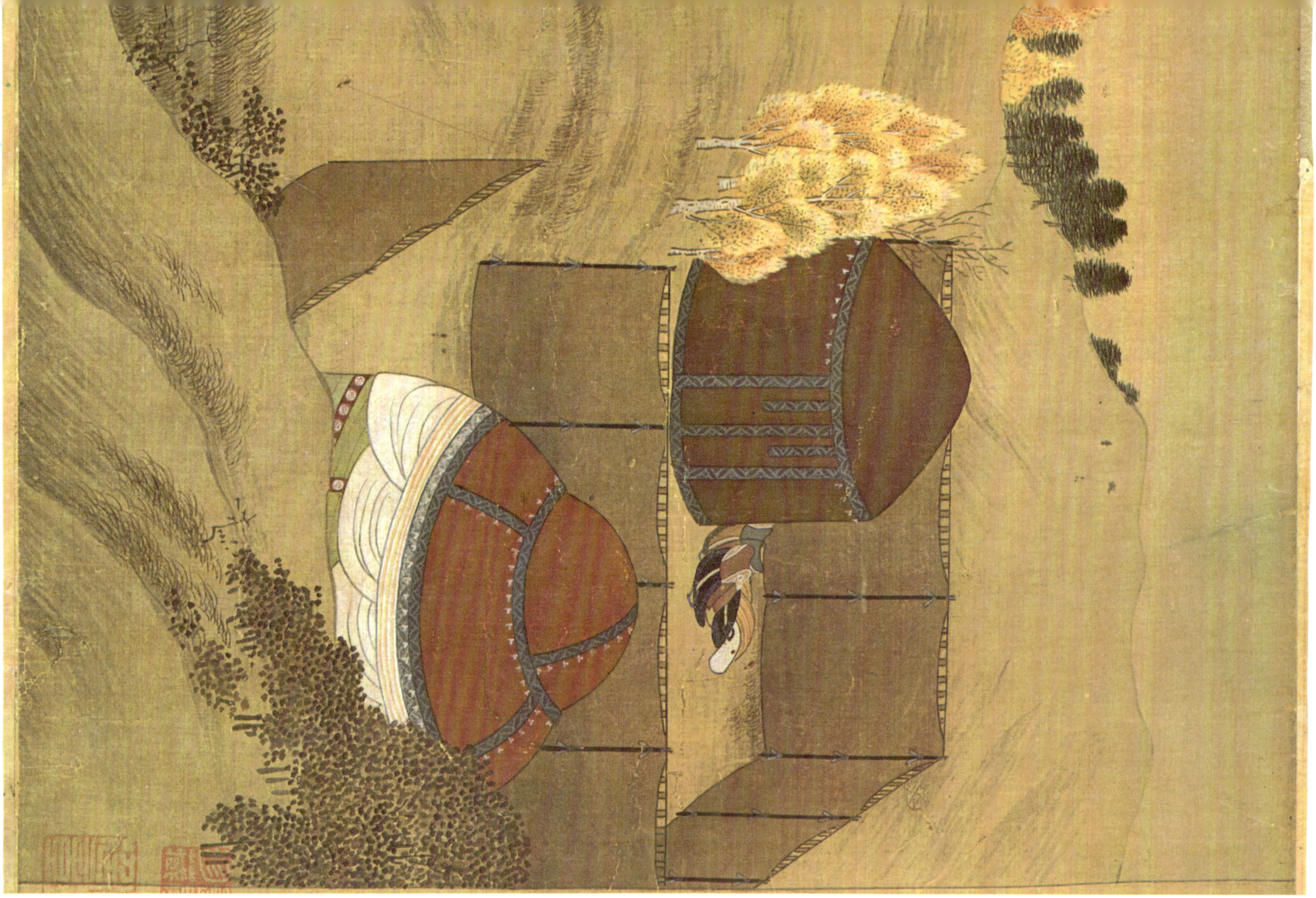

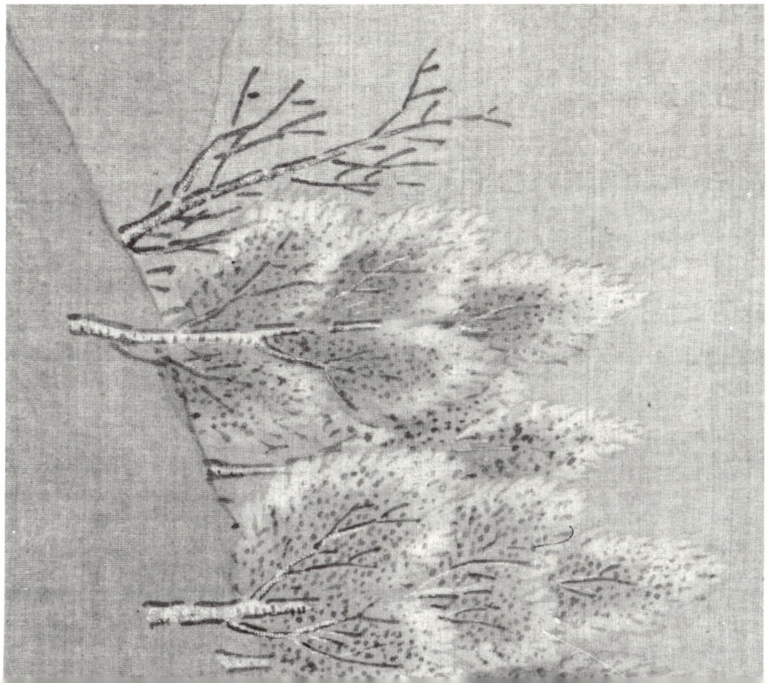

5 Encampment by a Stream

I sleep by water and sit on grass;
The wind that blows from China tears my clothing to pieces.
I clean my hair with mutton fat, but it is seldom combed.
*The collar of my lambskin robe is buttoned on the left;**
The fox lapels and badger sleeves are rank-smelling.
By day I wear these clothes, by night I sleep in them.
The felt screens are constantly being moved, since there is no fixed abode;
How long my days and nights are—they never seem to pass.

* Barbarian-style.

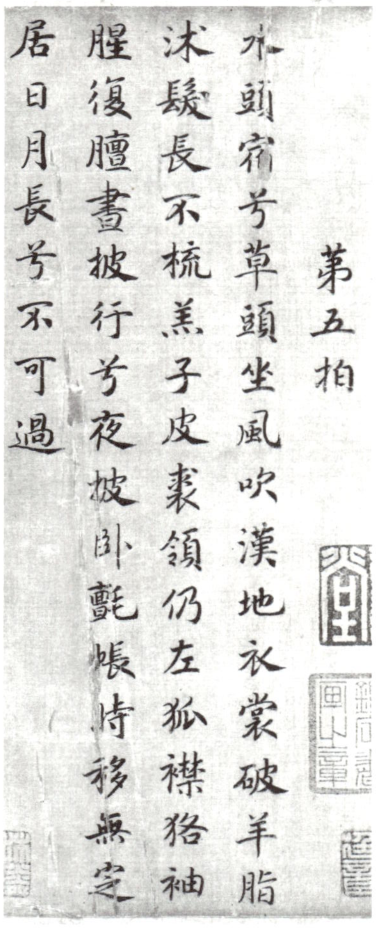

第五拍
氺頭宿兮草頭坐風吹漢地衣裳破羊脂
沐髮長不梳羔子皮裘領仍左狐襟貉袖
腥復膻晝披行兮夜披卧氈帳時移無定
居日月長兮不可過

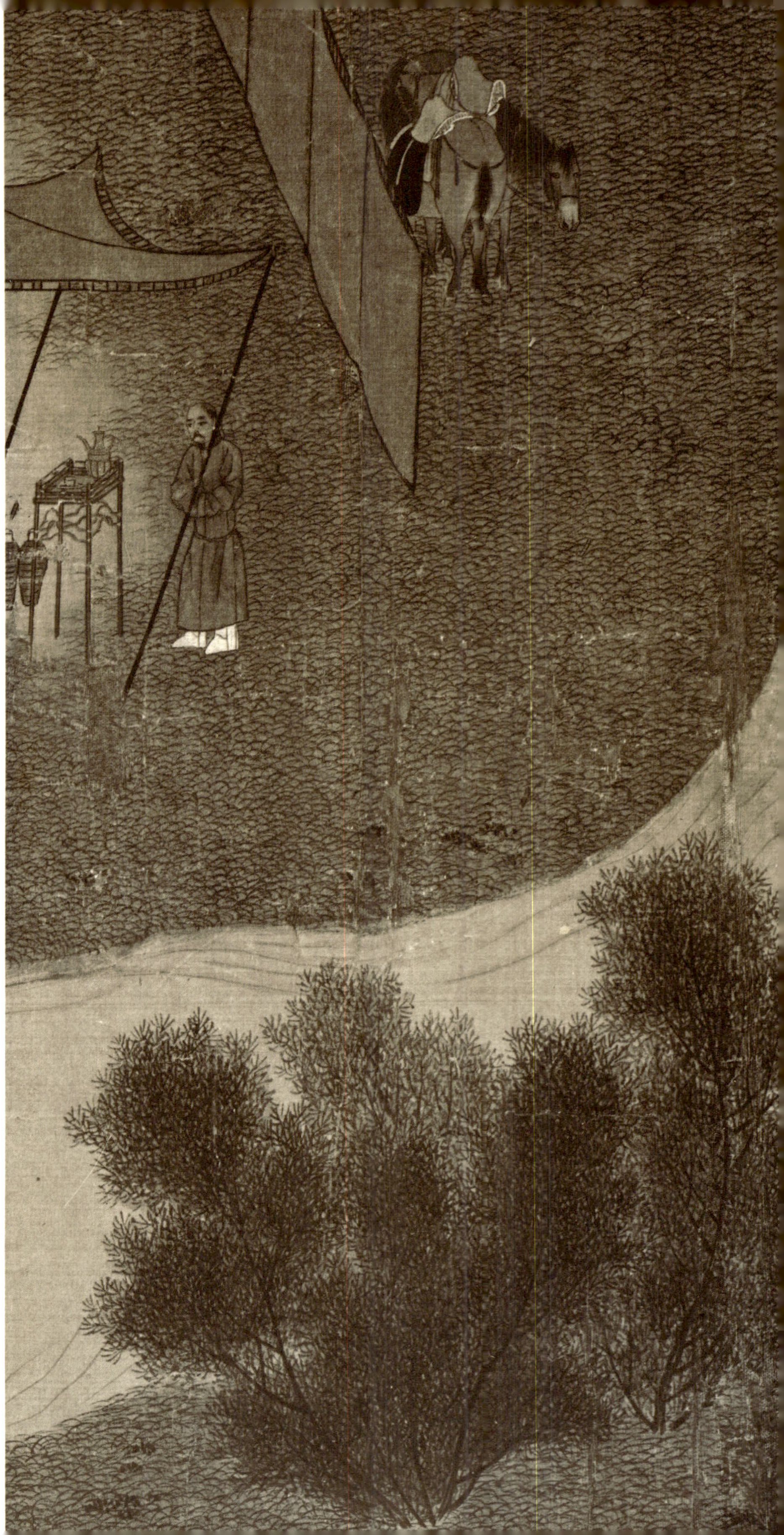

The prince and his unhappy wife are again at table; a ewer of wine in its warming bowl is ready on the lacquered serving table. At the left, behind a screen, food is being prepared: unleavened bread is being made and joints of mutton boil in one of the iron caldrons. To many Chinese, mutton has a most unpleasant odor, and one may imagine the cooking fires being fueled in part by mutton fat or animal dung. Grease and smells are among Wen-chi's chief complaints.

In detail after detail the artist evinces his knowledge of the nomads. The man walking from the cooking area shows us how this horse-riding people managed its long robes on less than formal occasions. The excellent traction wheels of the baggage carts show us their method of construction. The tribe's furled banners and stacked drums are described in the *History of Liao* as emblems of the Khitan ruler (Introduction, note 11). The drawing of the grass and willows recalls the work of Chao Ta-nien (active about 1070–1100) and Li T'ang (active about 1110–40); it is also close to the drawing in some other mid-twelfth-century Academy landscapes that followed in Li T'ang's tradition (Fong, *Sung and Yuan Paintings*, pages 64–65).

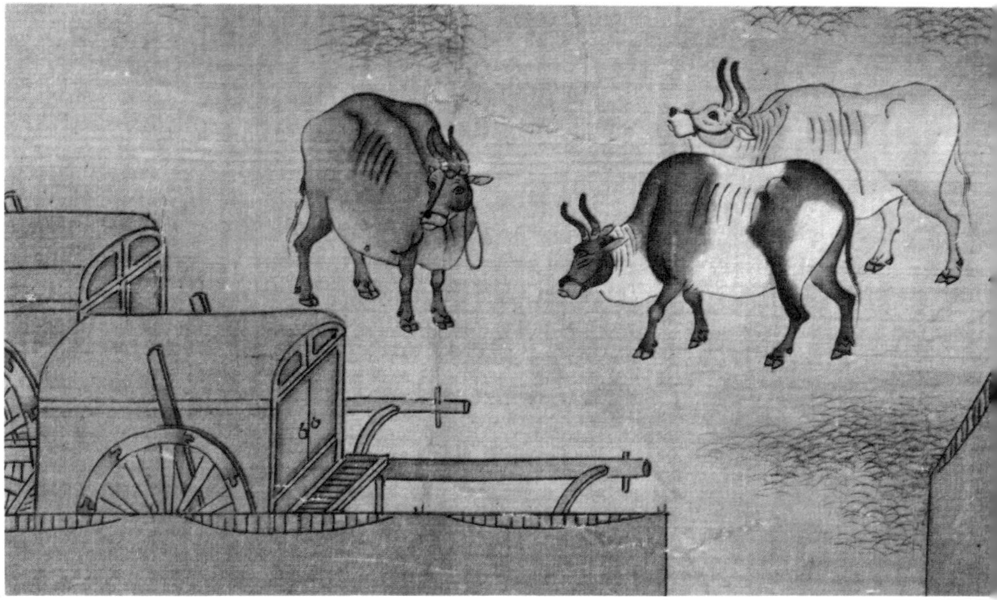

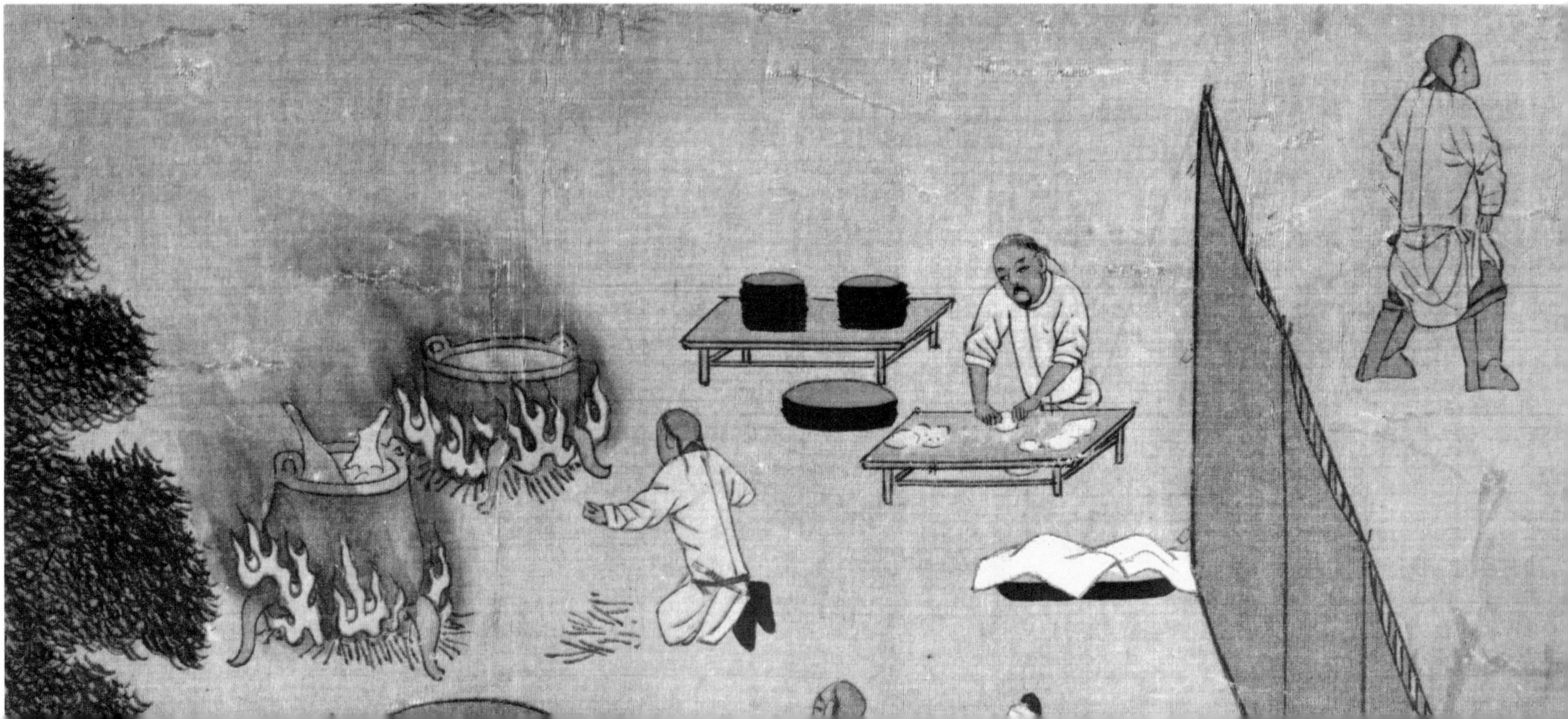

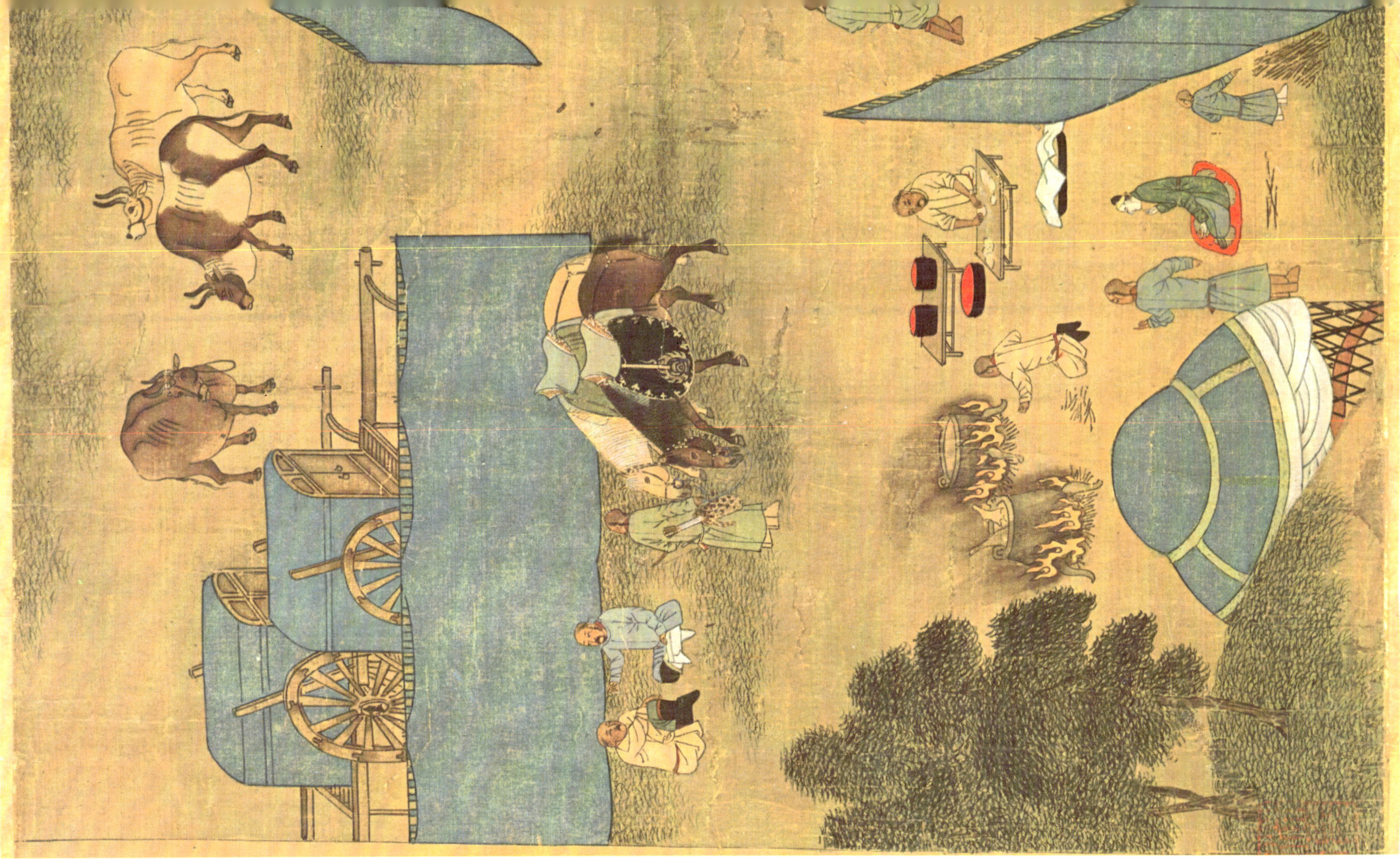

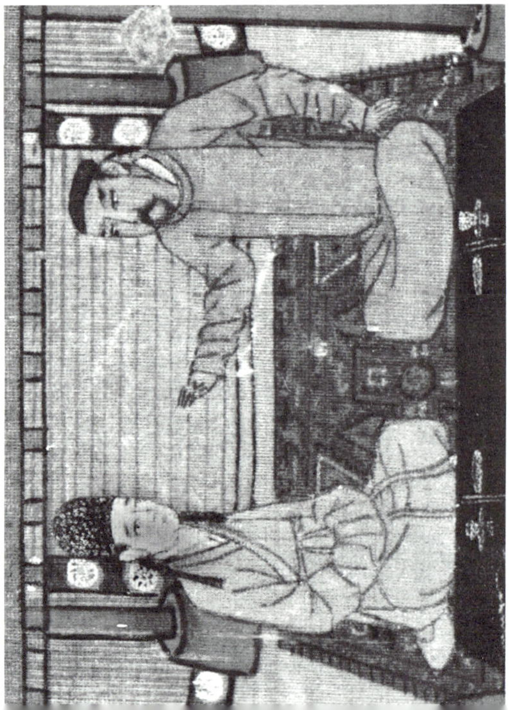

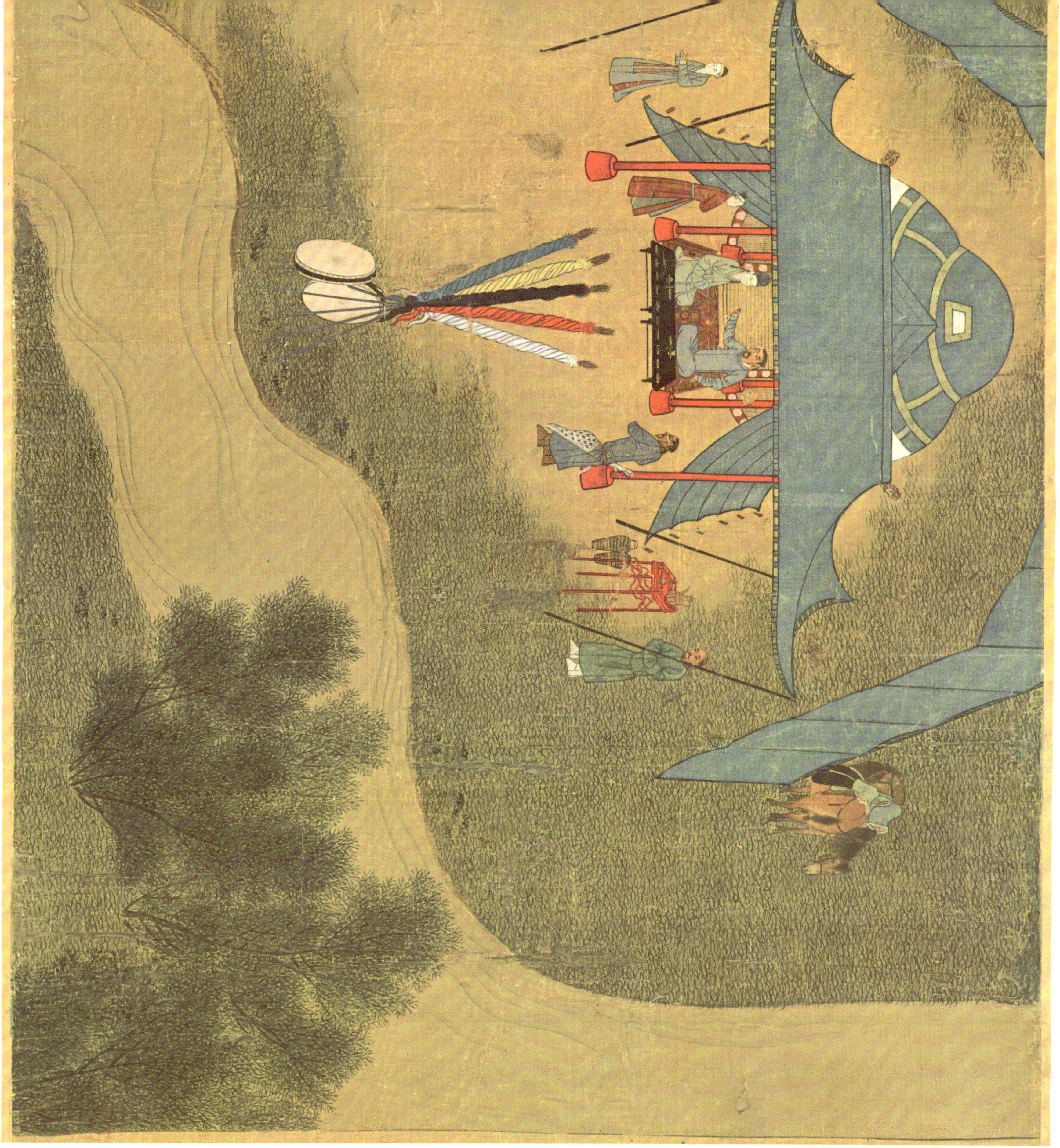

6 The Constellation of the Dipper

I resent it that spring is so short here;
In the nomad land there are few flowers or willows.
Who knows if heaven and earth have not been turned upside down?
Here we see the Great Dipper in the south.
Since our names, sounds, and signals are wholly different,
All day and all year I keep my mouth closed.
"Yes" and "no" and accepting and giving things away all depend on finger gestures;
For expressing our feelings, speech has become less useful than the hand.

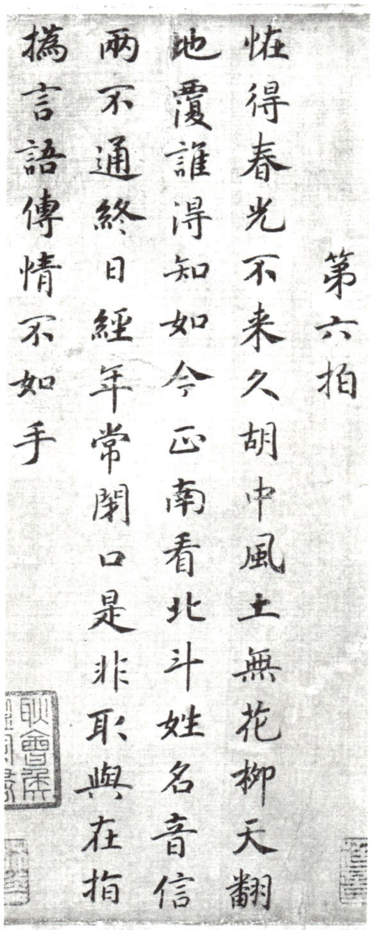
第六拍
恠得春光不来久胡中風土無花柳天翻
地覆誰得知如今正南看北斗姓名音信
兩不通終日經年常閉口是非取與在指
撝言語傳情不如手

While the poem describes the sufferings of one bereft of directional sense and spoken communication, the painter again—as in the fourth scene—seizes on concrete imagery. Here the prince joins Wen-chi and happily shares in her viewing of the constellation with his hand, rather than with speech.

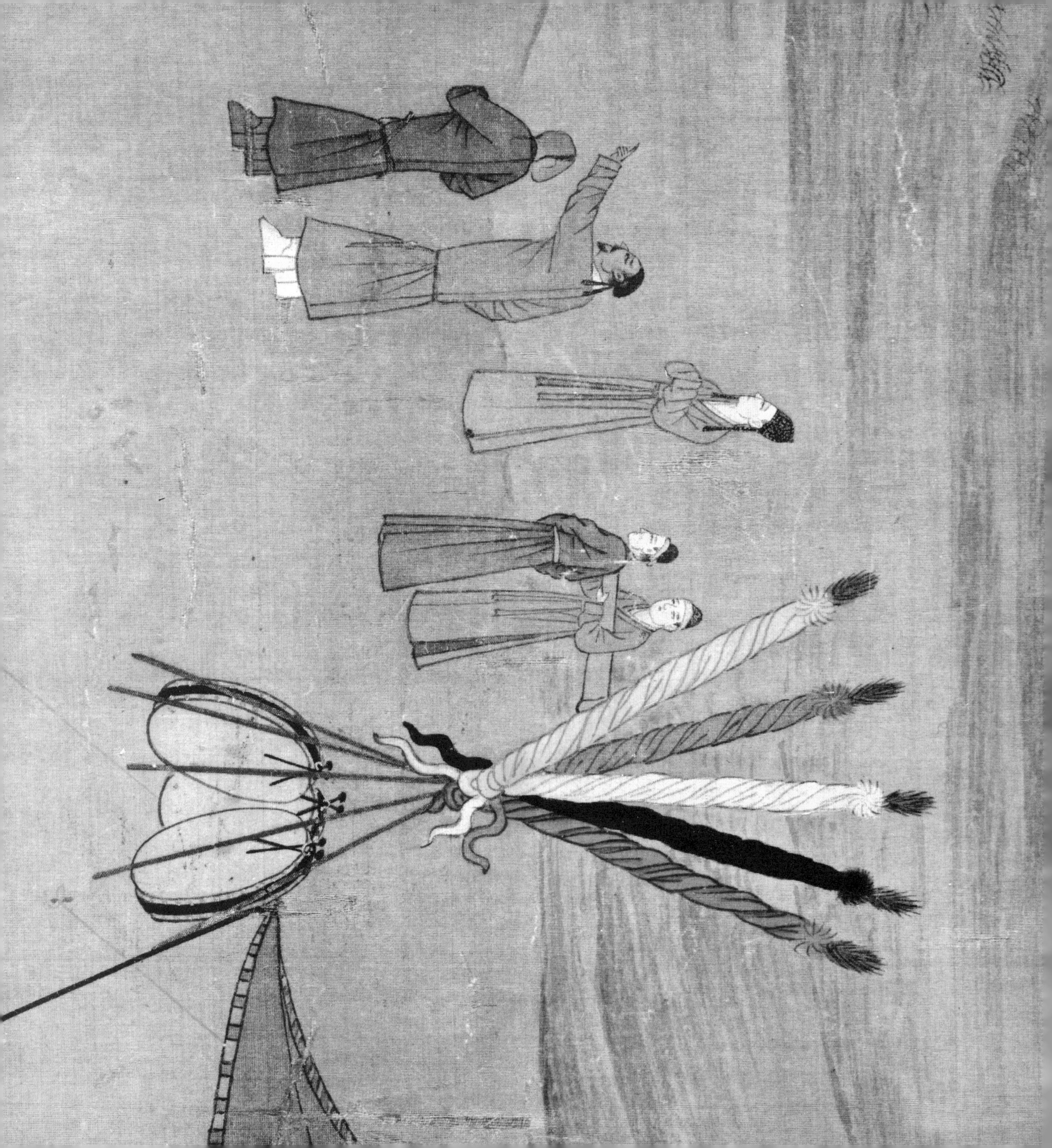

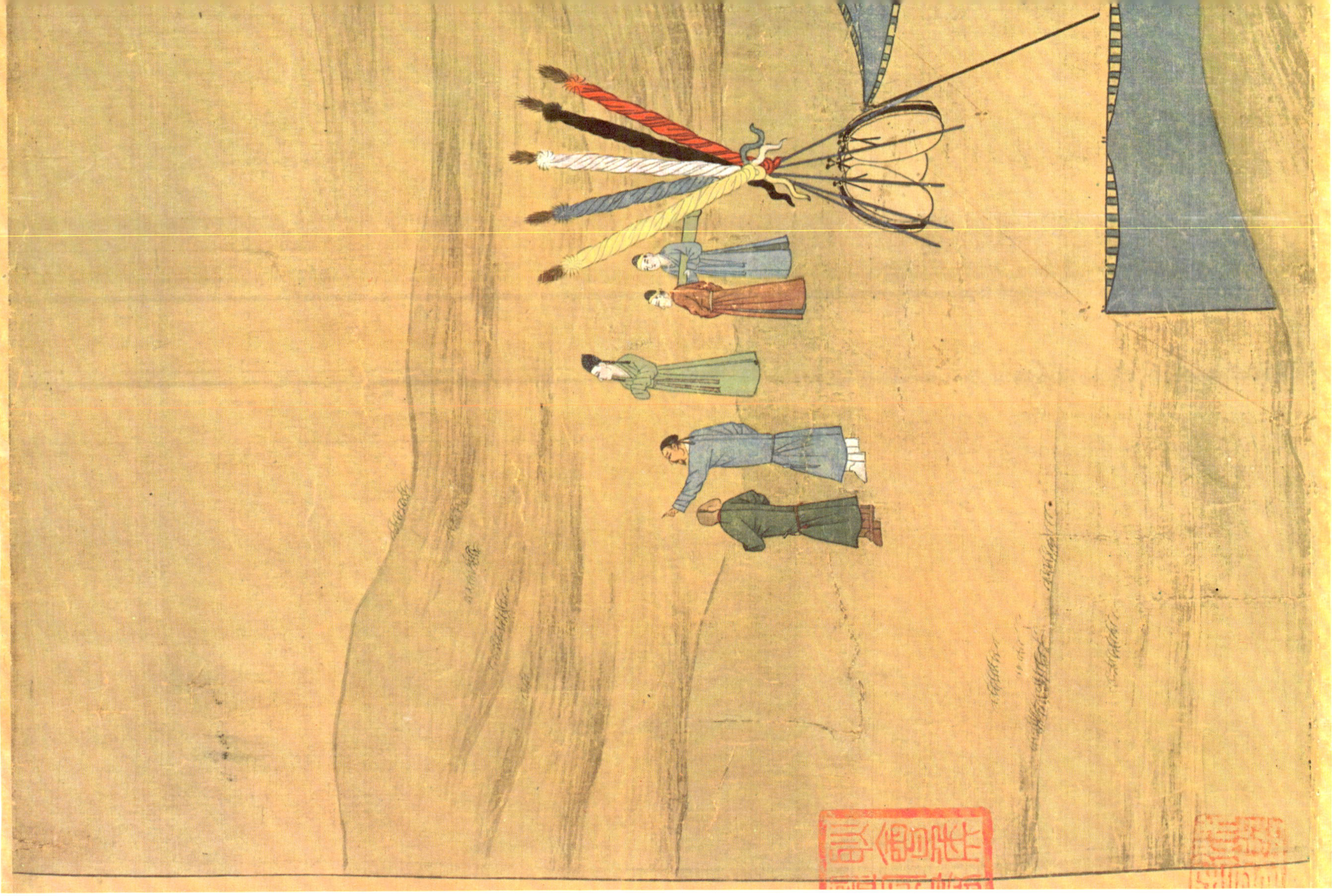

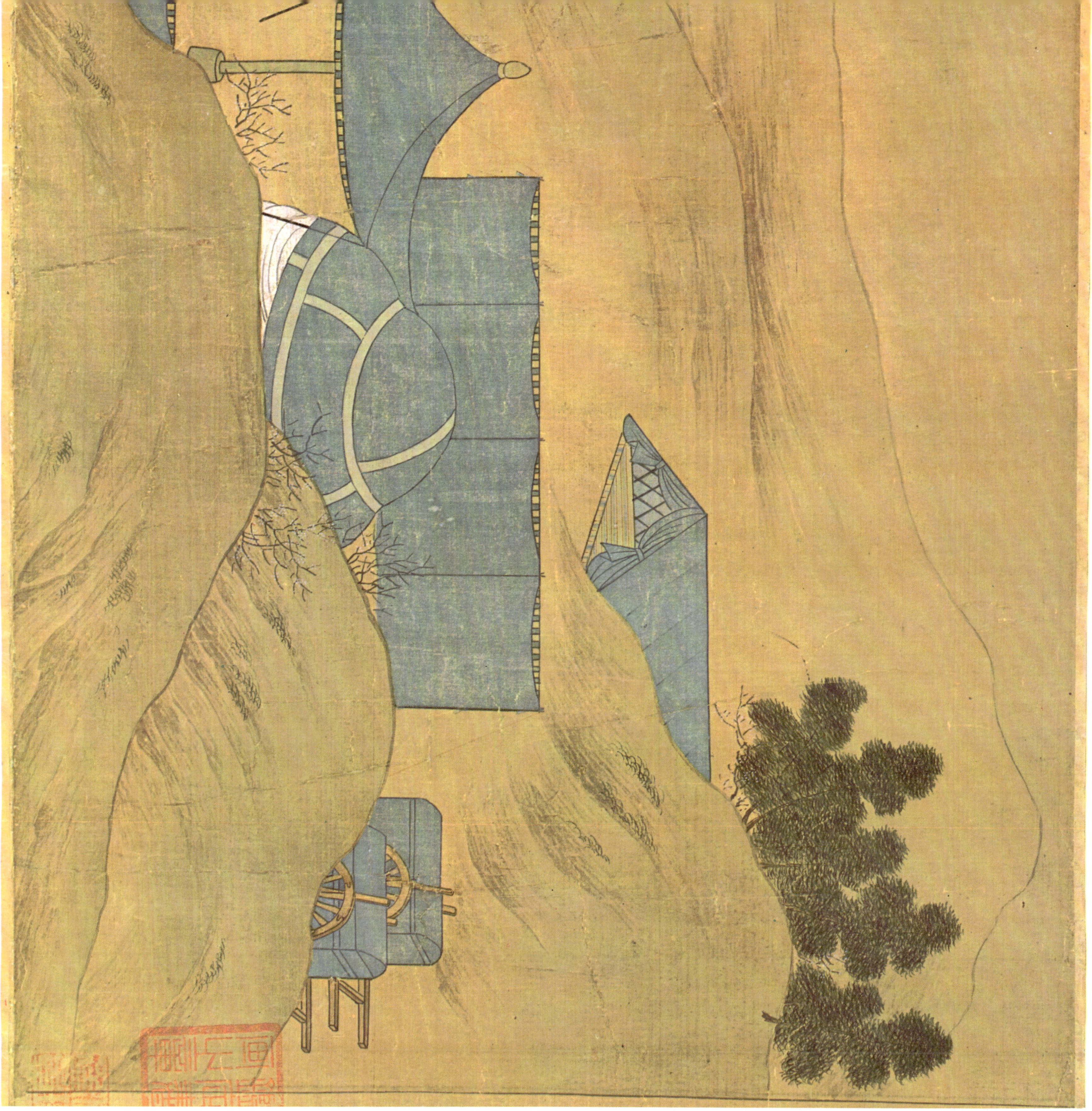

7 Concert on the Steppe

Their men and women both carry bows and arrows;
Their border ponies and native sheep lie about in frost and sleet.
How can there be freedom for me to take a single step in any direction?
Neither living stealthily nor begging for an early death can be my true wish.
I listen to the pi-li *of Ch'iu-tzu* in sadness;*
The p'i-p'a *of Sui-yeh† makes mournful sounds in the deep of the night.*
Through the cloudless night the moon rises high in the sky;
Oh, but I must see my home town again!

*Han dynasty name for a region in modern Sinkiang province.
†City west of Lake Baikal in Central Asia.

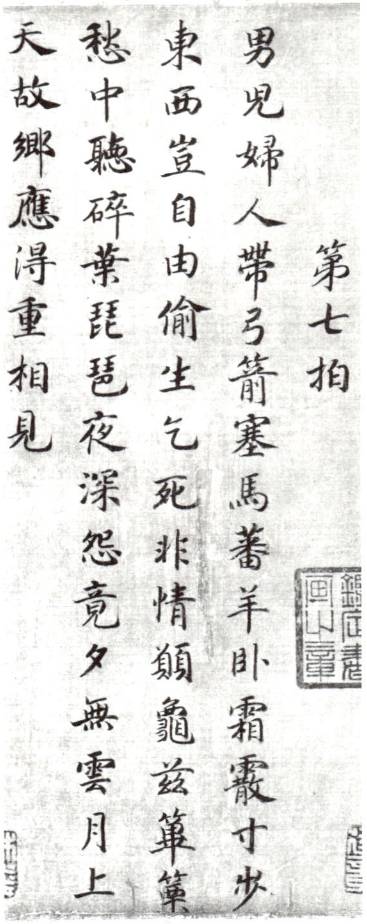
第七拍
男兒婦人帶弓箭塞馬蕃羊卧霜霰寸步
東西豈自由偷生乞死非情願龜茲篳篥
愁中聽碎葉琵琶夜深怨竟夕無雲月上
天故鄉應渇重相見

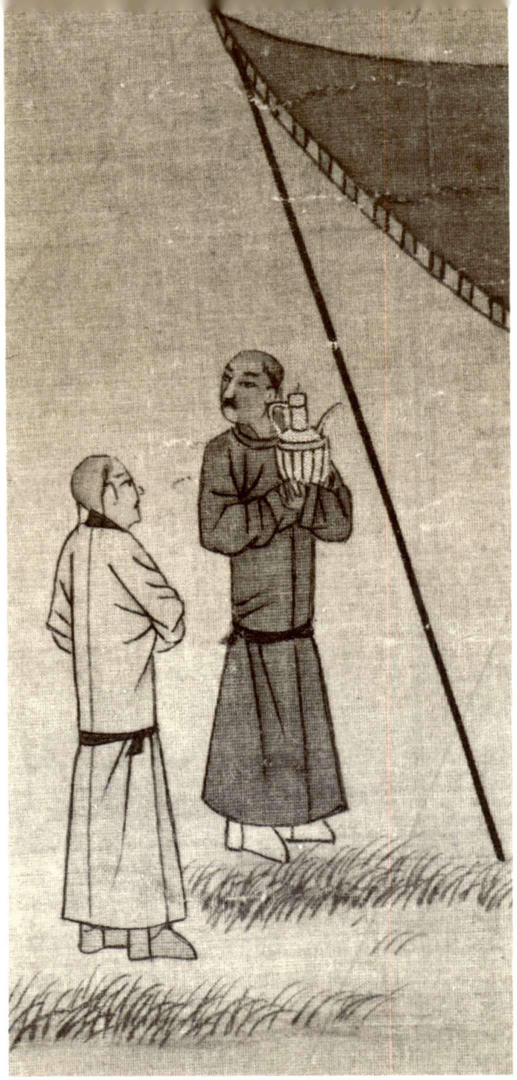

Disdained though they were by the Chinese, the nomads did not lack arts of their own. Here, Wen-chi names two of the instruments she hears, the *pi-li*, a horn, and the lutelike *p'i-p'a* (the latter played by the musician seated beside the empty cushion), and mentions their supposed places of origin in Central Asia. Historically, the *p'i-p'a* attained favor in China during the T'ang period—the time of the poems—long after Wen-chi's day. While the musicians perform, a platter of mutton arrives from the cooking area. The wine steward holds a beautiful ewer of Liao type. The prince is, as usual, vigorous and animated, but Wen-chi again looks downcast.

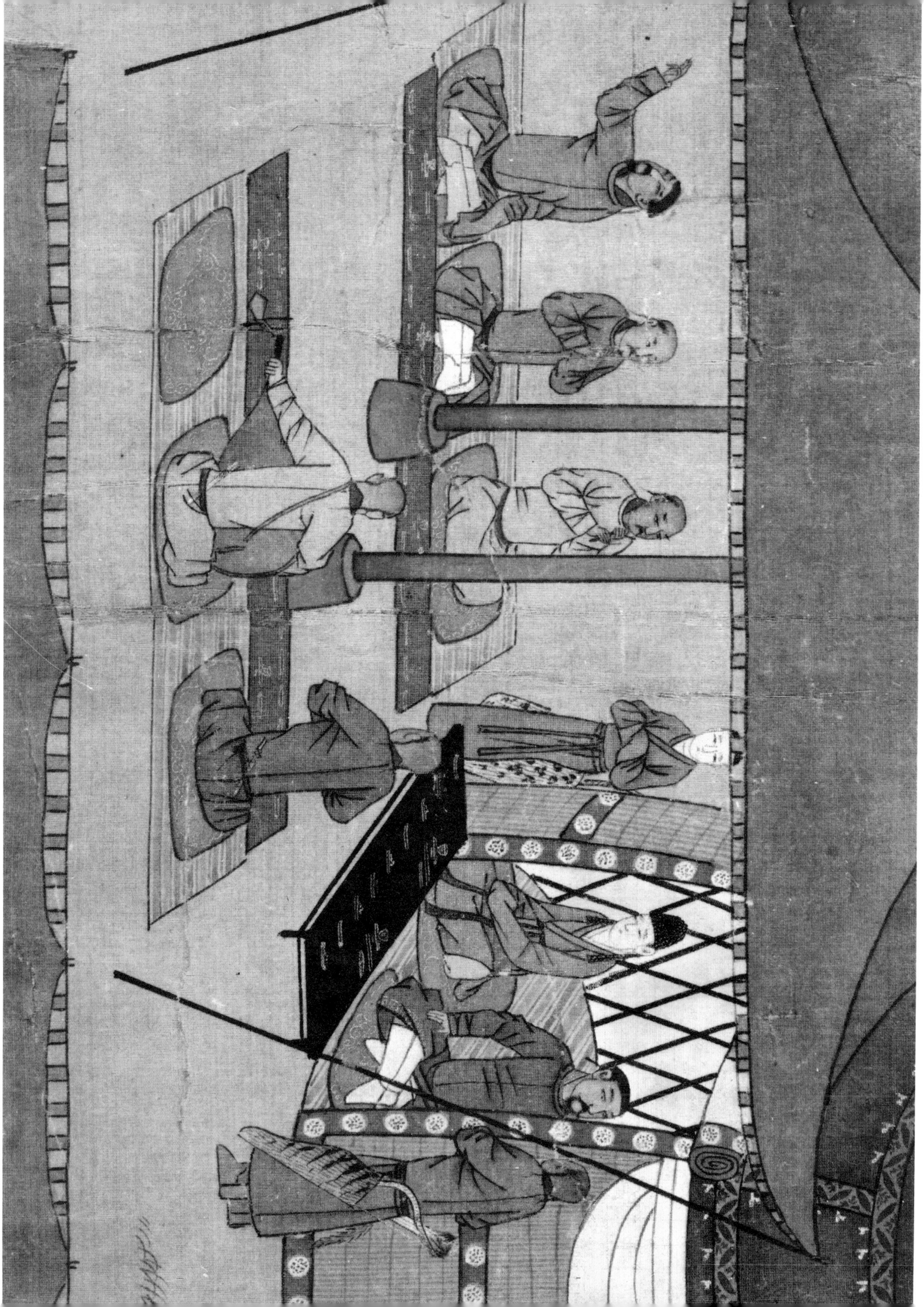

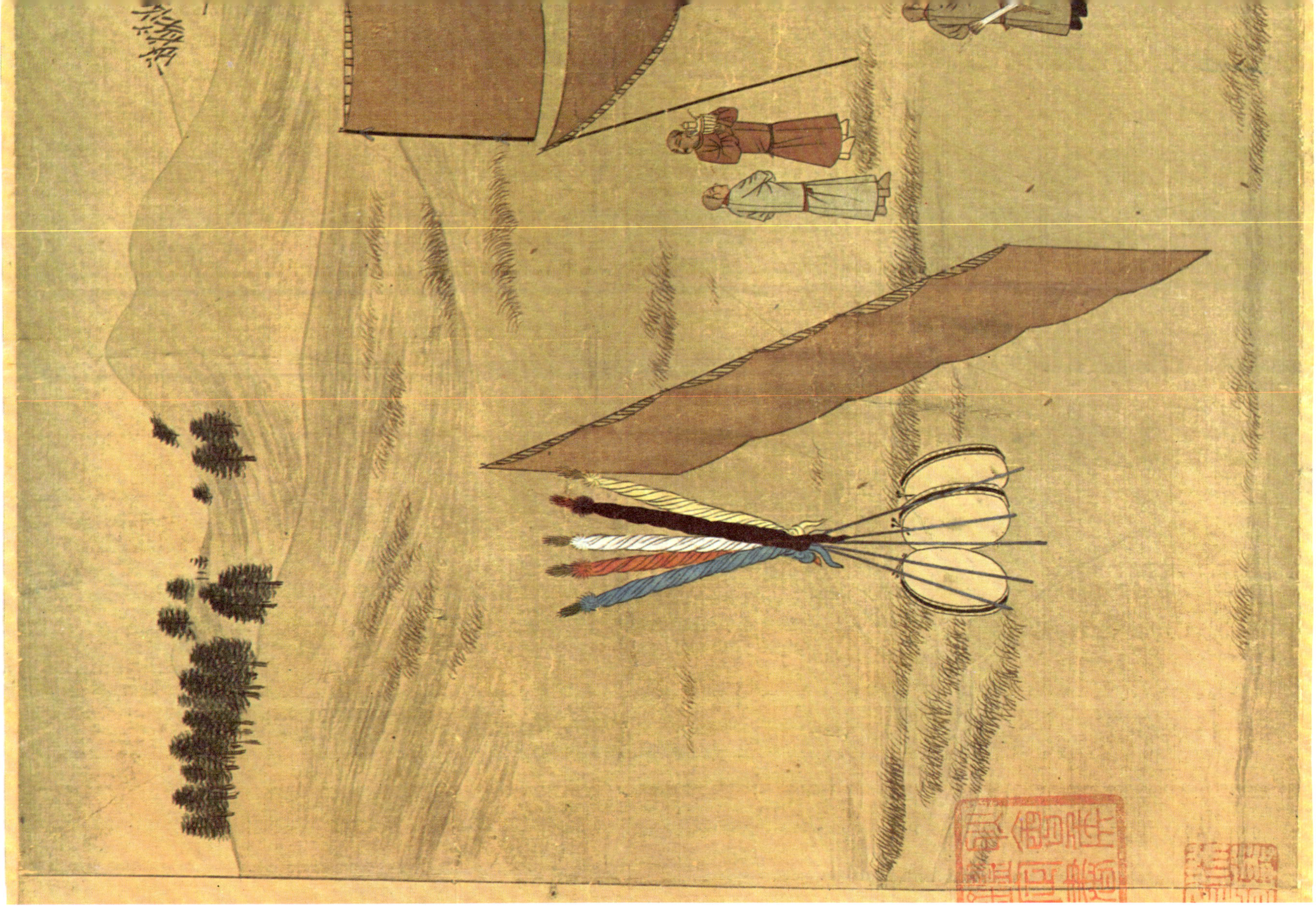

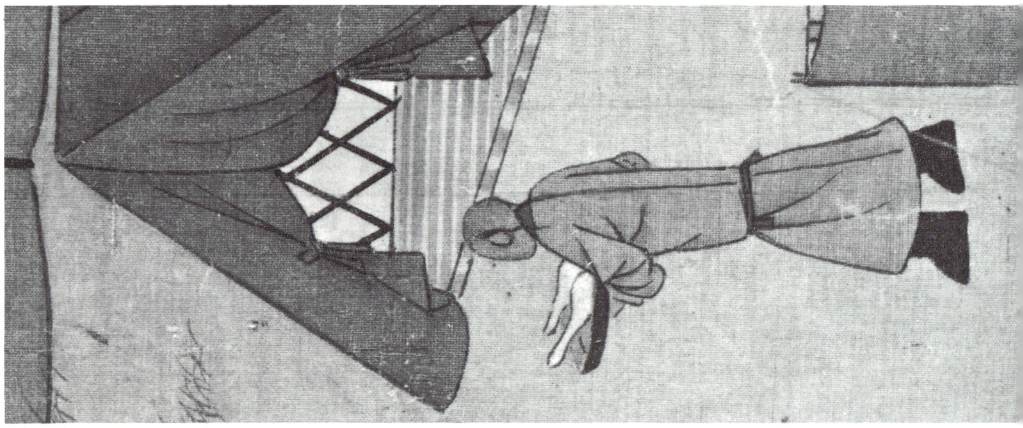

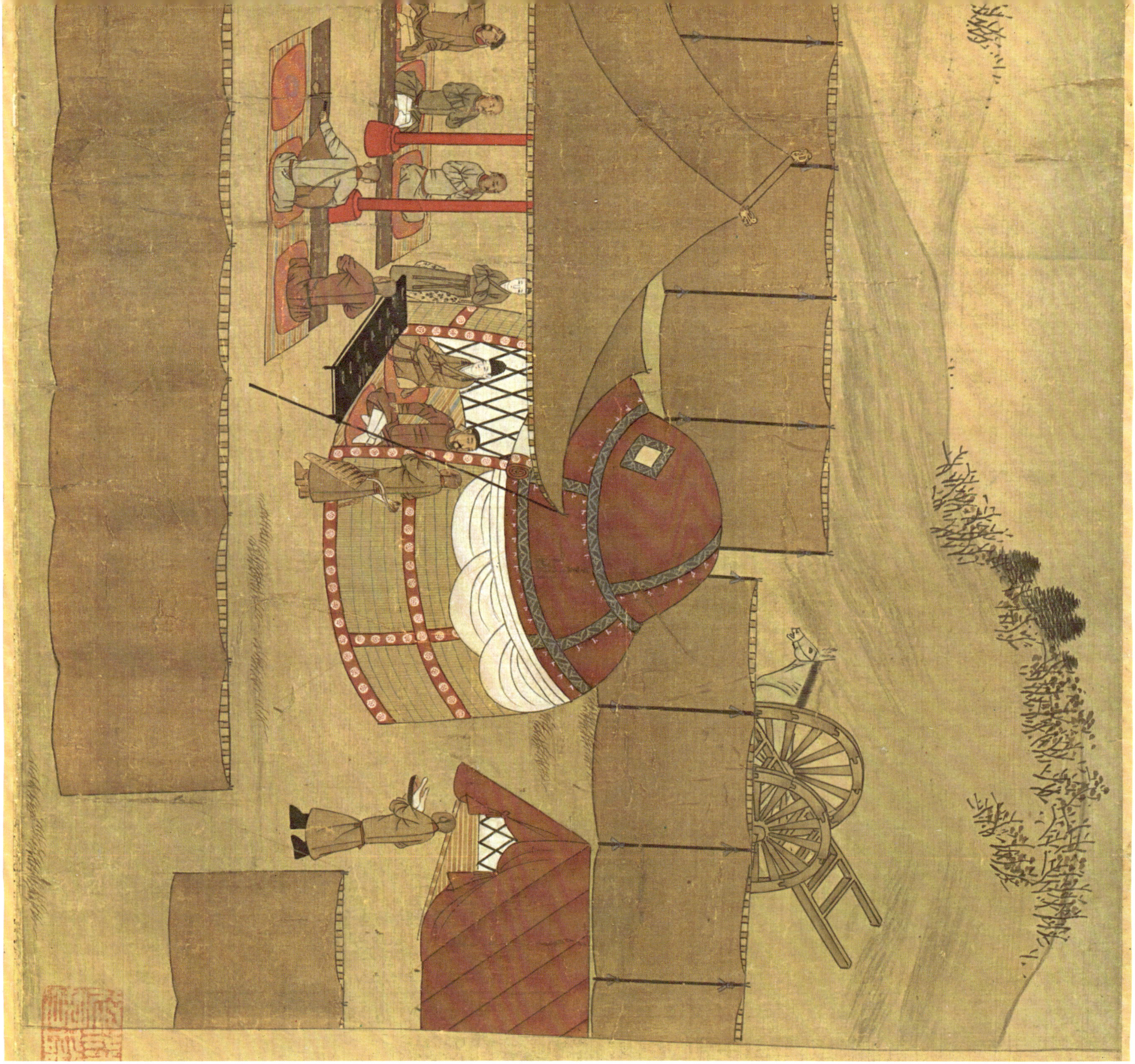

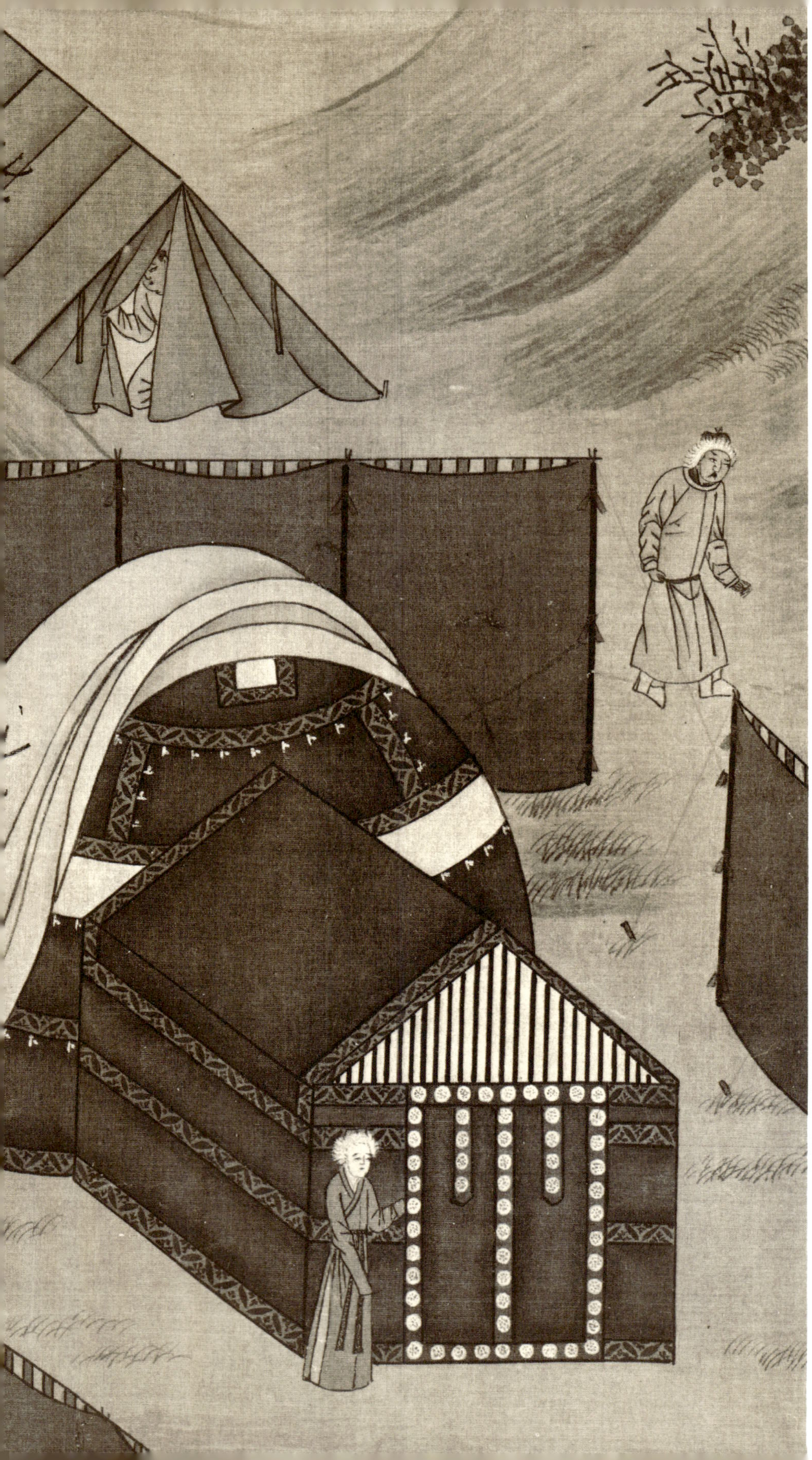

8 Dawn

I remember the past, when I was an attractive but spoiled child at home.
From afar was obtained a rare bird, which I tamed.
Now, lost and abandoned, I think of my old home;
I regret that I did not release my bird to the forest.
The north wind whistles and the cold sun sets;
The lonely river of stars hangs above, until dawn comes again in the nomad sky.
Day and night I think of returning, but I cannot return;
My sorrowful heart, I think, must be like that bird in its cage.

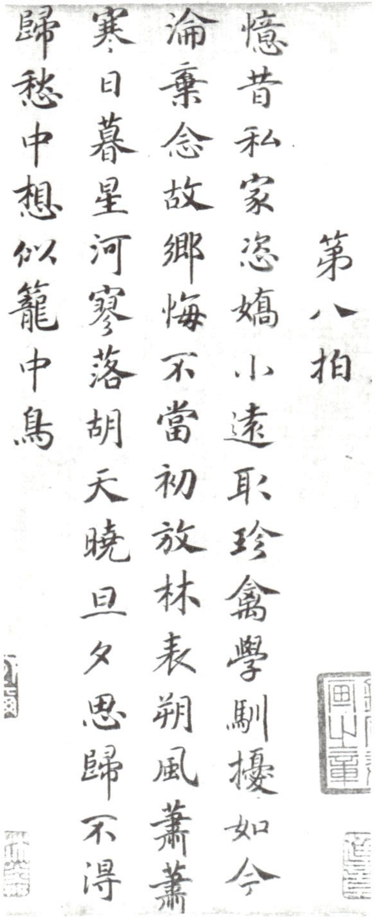

第八拍

憶昔私家恣嬌小遠取珍禽學馴擾如今
淪棄念故鄉悔不當初放林表朔風蕭蕭
寒日暮星河寥落胡天曉旦夕思歸不得
歸愁中想似籠中鳥

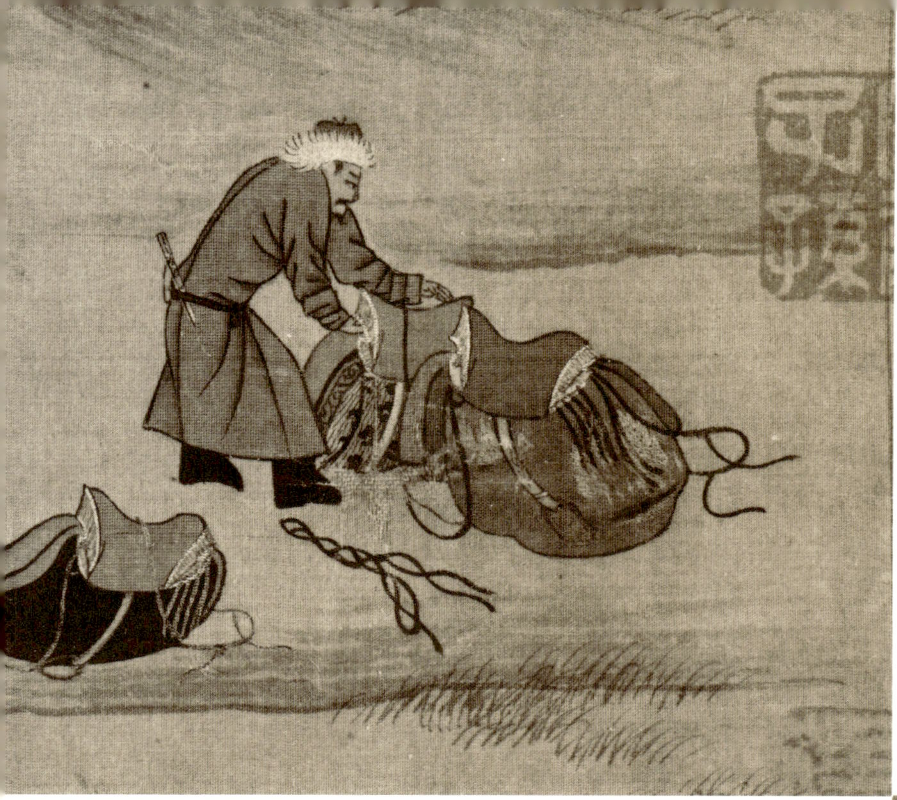

Developing the imagery of the caged bird, the painter conceals Wen-chi in a tightly closed tent, guarded by a female attendant. Dawn breaks. Tribesmen play reveille on drums and horns. Others come from their tents and prepare their horses.

The rousing sound of the *hua-chiao* (painted horn), made of bamboo and skin and played at dawn and dusk, echoes that of the *pi-li* in the seventh poem—all part of the alien environment that grates upon the sensibilities of the Chinese lady.

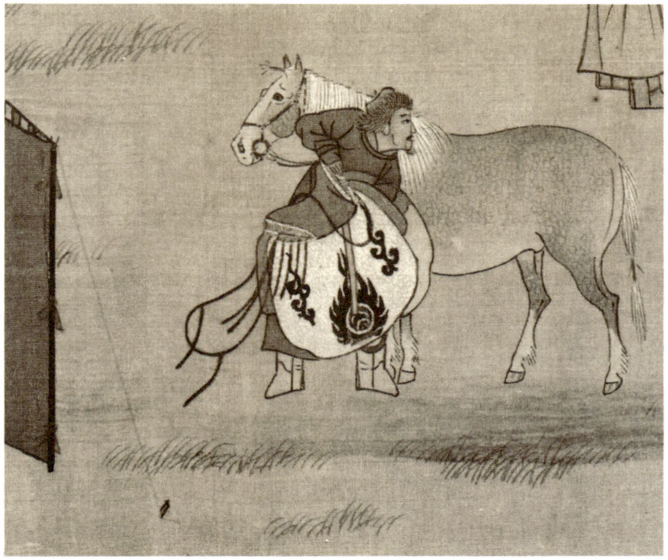

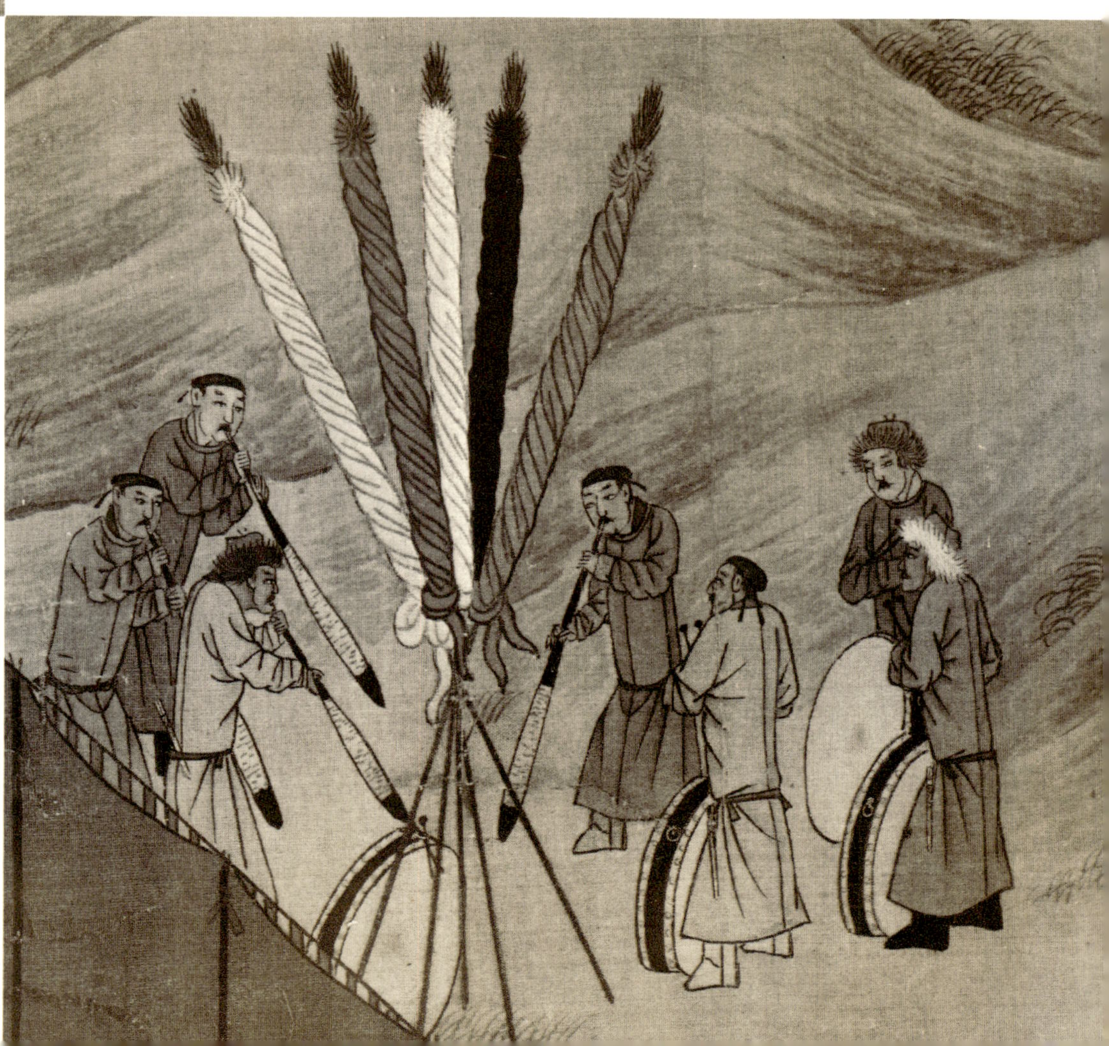

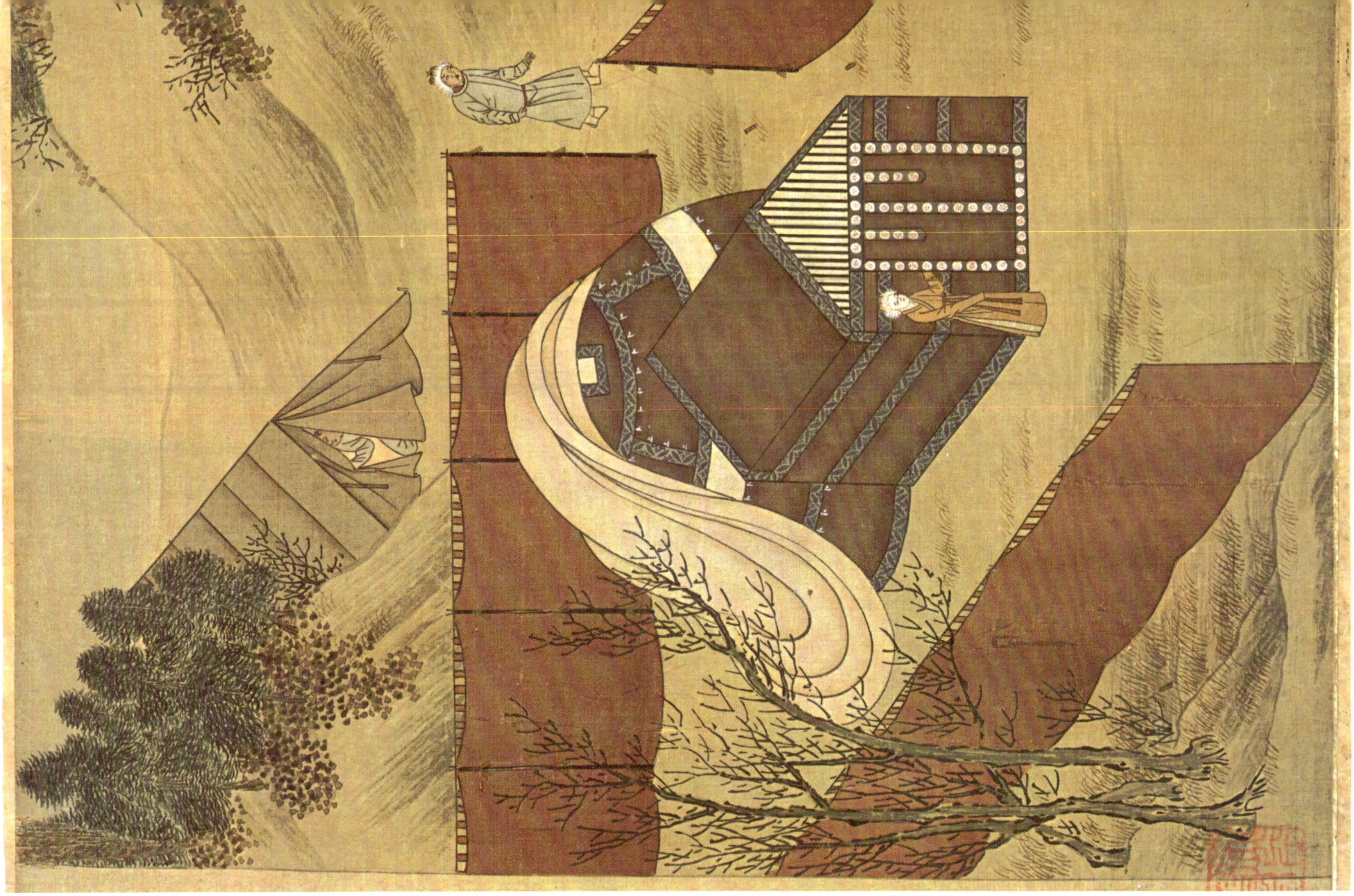

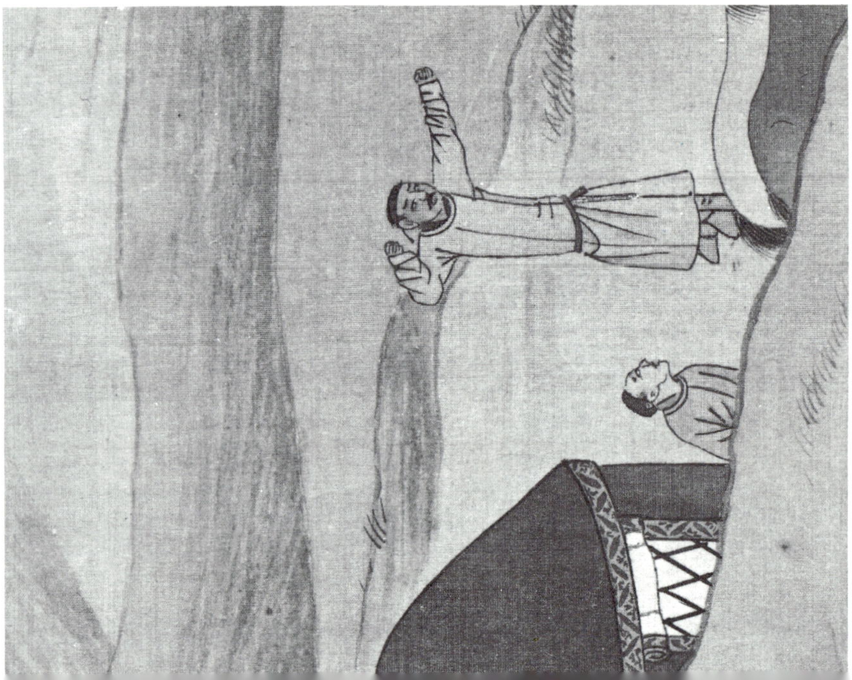

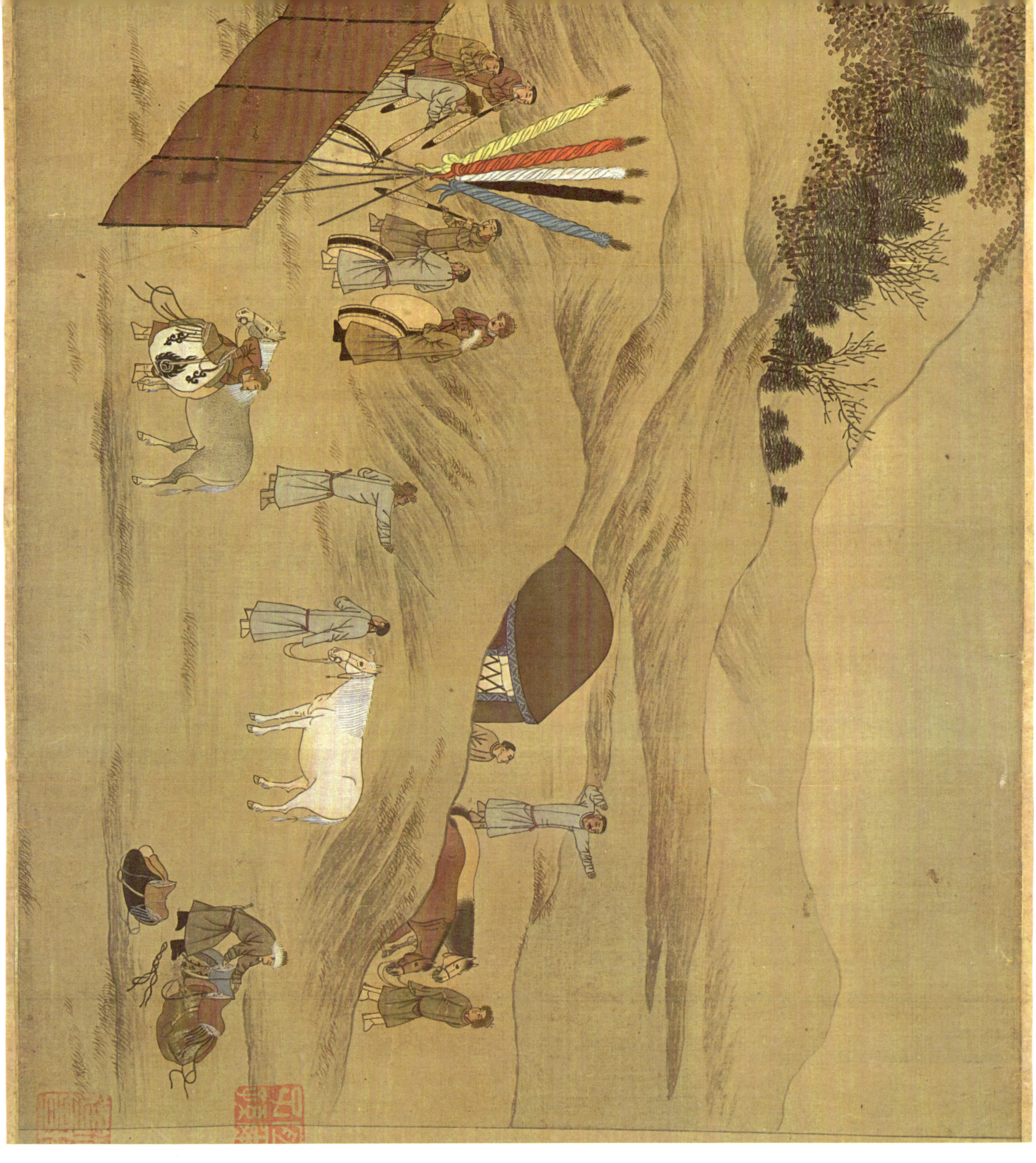

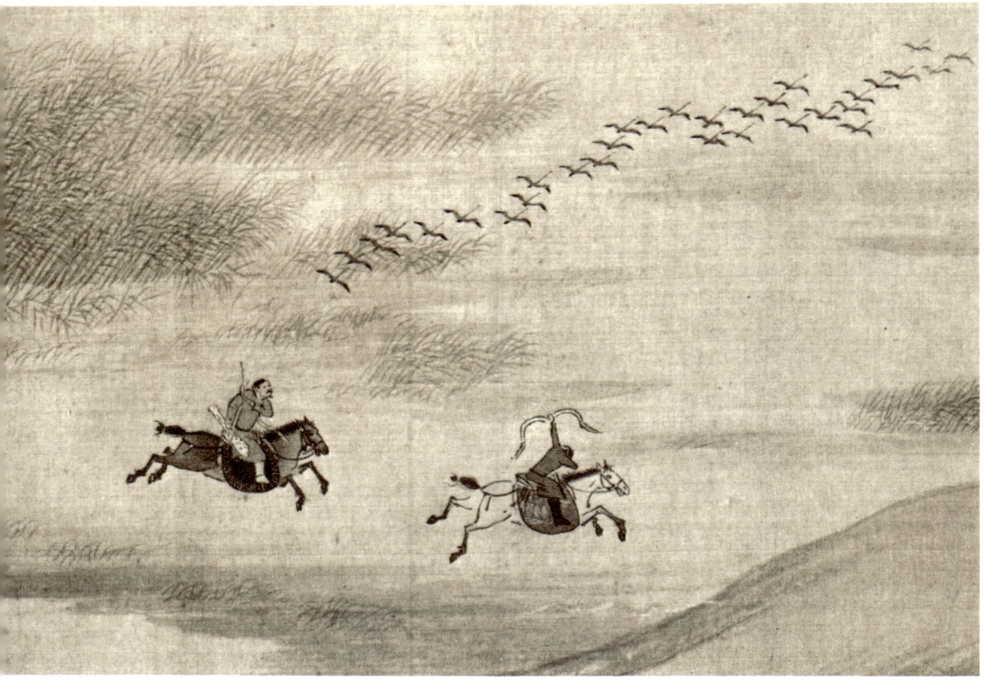

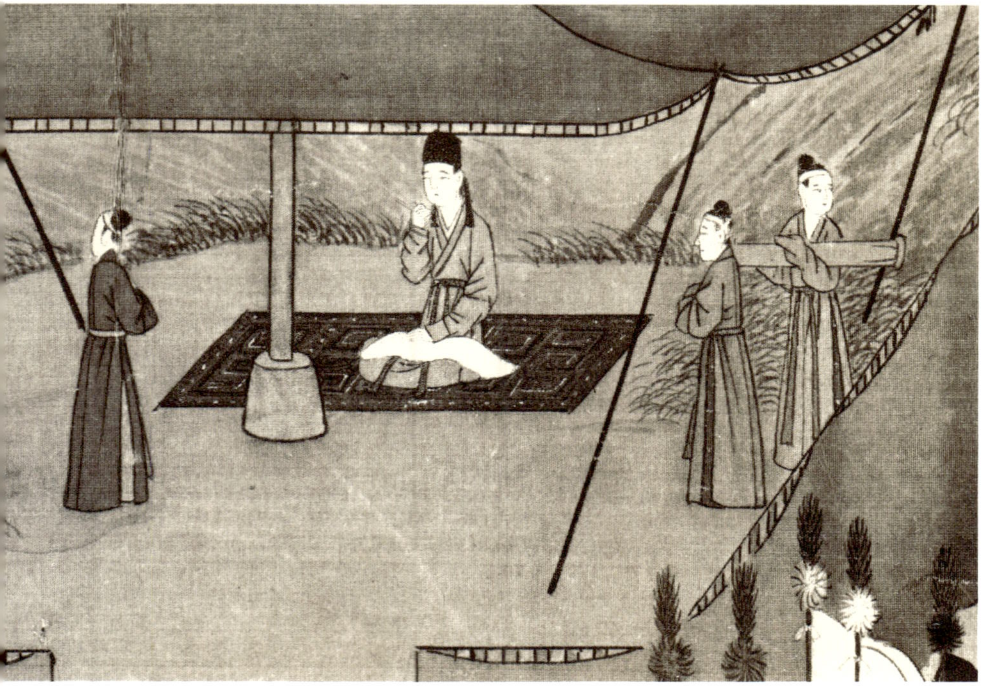

9 Writing Home

In the past, when Su Wu was questioned by the Khan,
It is said that the migrating geese knew how to carry a message.
Imitating Su Wu, I prick blood to write a letter;
In this letter I write a thousand and ten thousand grievances.
But the bearded barbarian youths are excellent horsemen;
They bend their bows and shoot flying birds, far and near.
Now the geese of the frontier are afraid of people;
How can I have my heart heard from these ends of the earth?

An official during the reign of Han Wu-ti (140–86 B.C.), Su Wu was sent as an envoy to the Huns, and was held prisoner by them. When the Khan reported to a later Chinese envoy that Su had died in his keeping, he was told that the Han emperor had received a message from Su carried by a goose.

Seated on a fine rug under a canopy, Wen-chi bites her finger to draw blood. But will she be able to find a winged messenger—and, having found one, will it get through to her homeland? The thought is answered by the scene in the distance, where two of the tribesmen engage in a familiar nomad skill: shooting wildfowl while riding at a flying gallop.

The tribe's banners, for a change, are unfurled, perhaps indicating that this is a settled campsite.

第九拍

當日蘇武單于問道是賓鴻解傳信學他
刺血寫得書書上千重萬重恨驕胡少年
能走馬彎弓射飛無遠近遂令邊鴈轉怕
人絕域何由達方寸

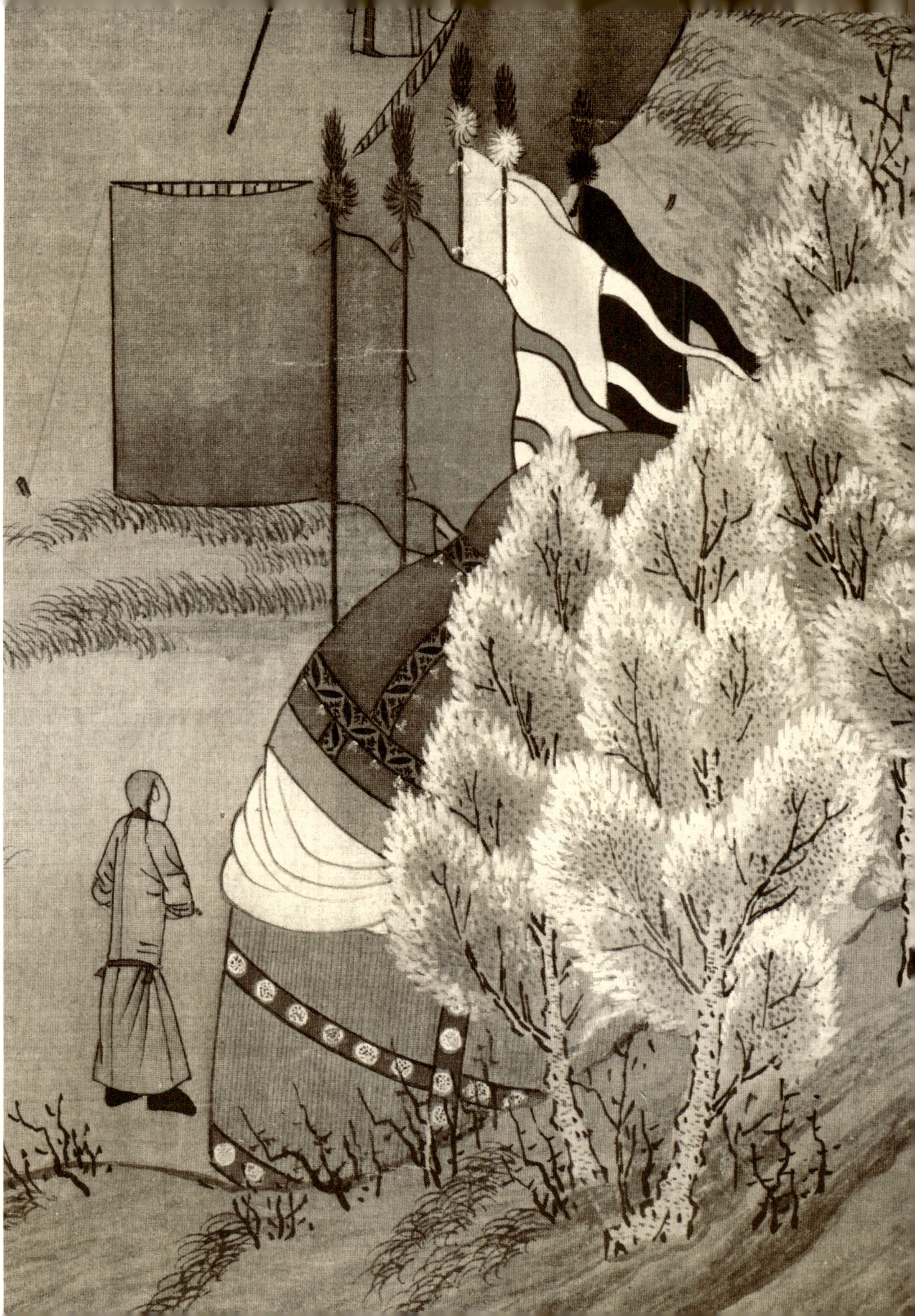

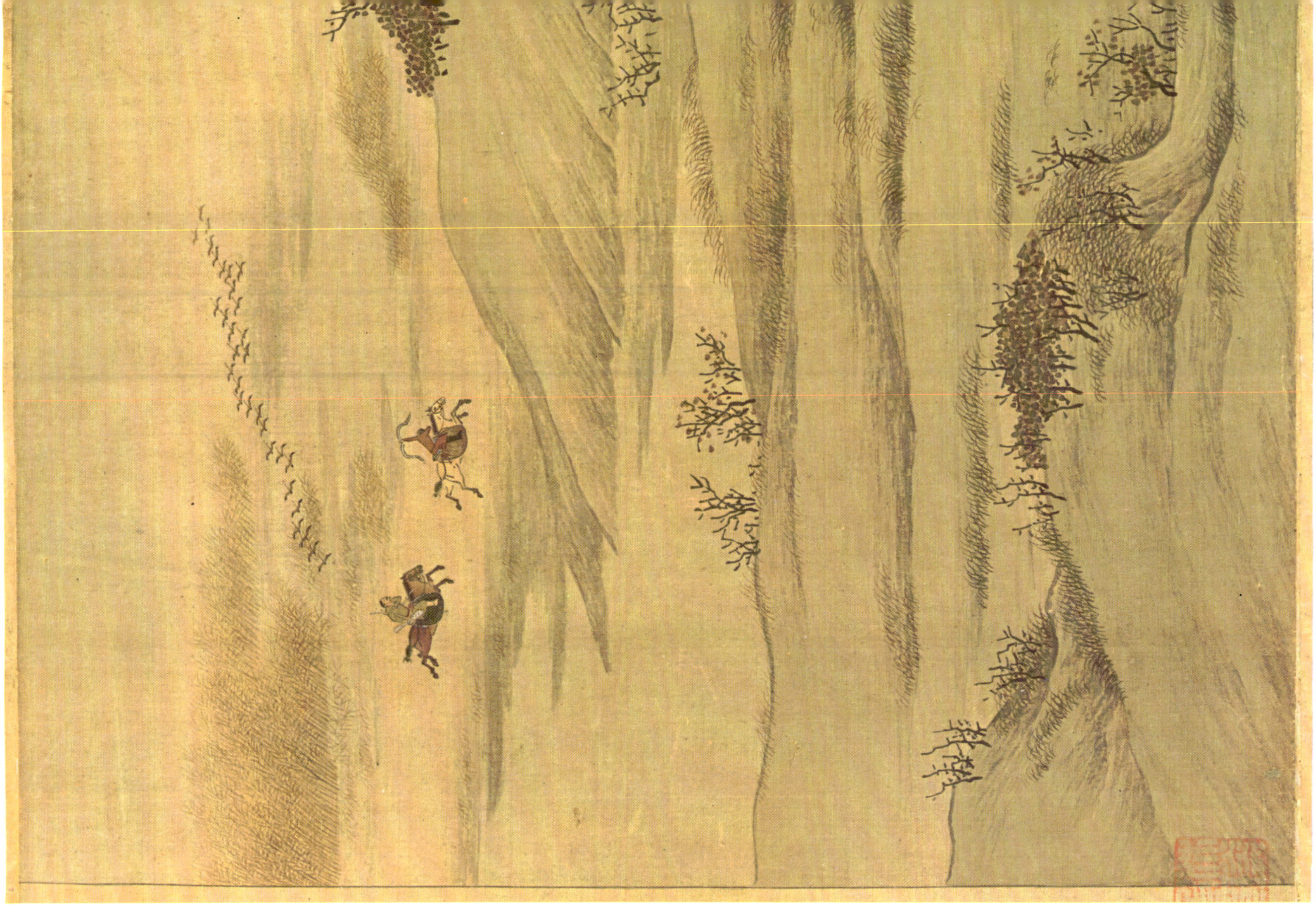

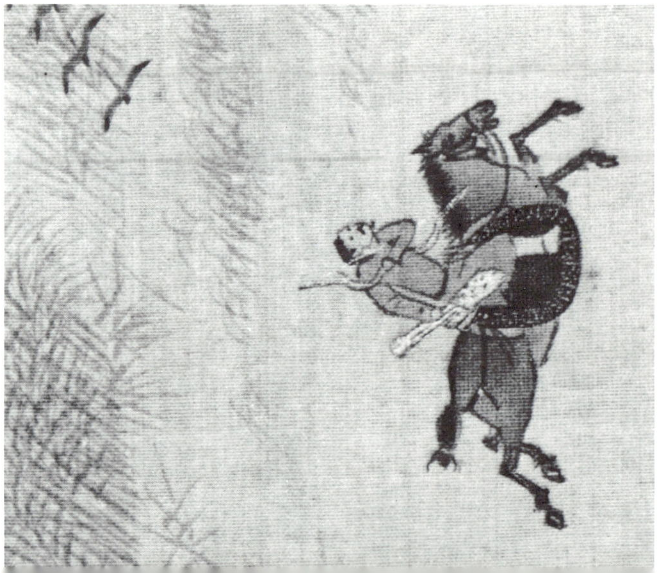

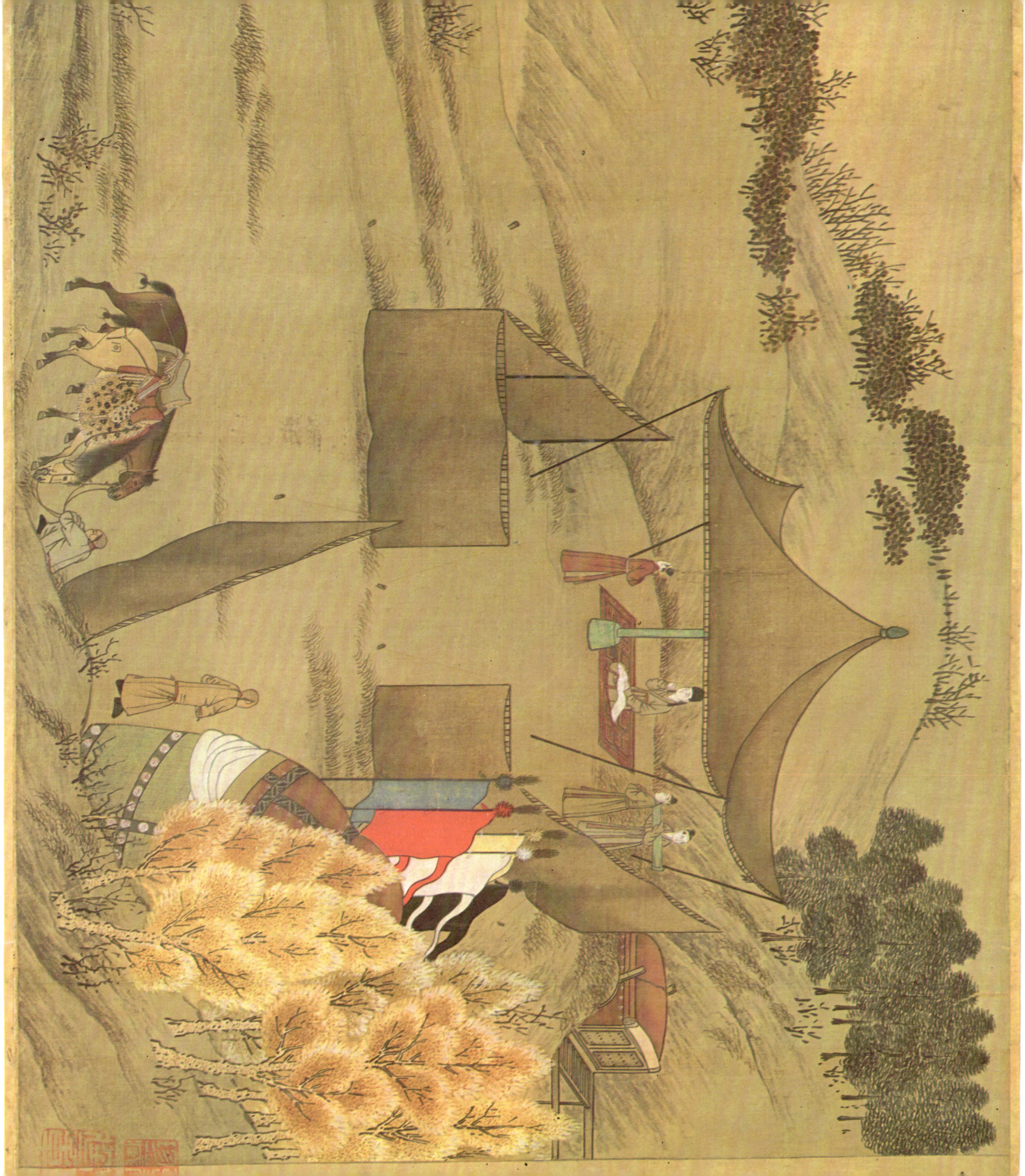

10 A Child Is Born

How I am grieved by the indignities I have suffered, and revolted by
rank smells;
How I despise the nomad land and hate the nomad sky!
When I became pregnant with a barbarian child, I wanted to kill myself,
Yet once I bore it, I found the love of mother and child.
His looks are strange, and his speech is different, yet my hate turns
into love;
Deep inside, I feel the tug of my heartstring.
Morning and evening he is with me:
How can I not pity that which my womb has borne and my hand
nurtured?

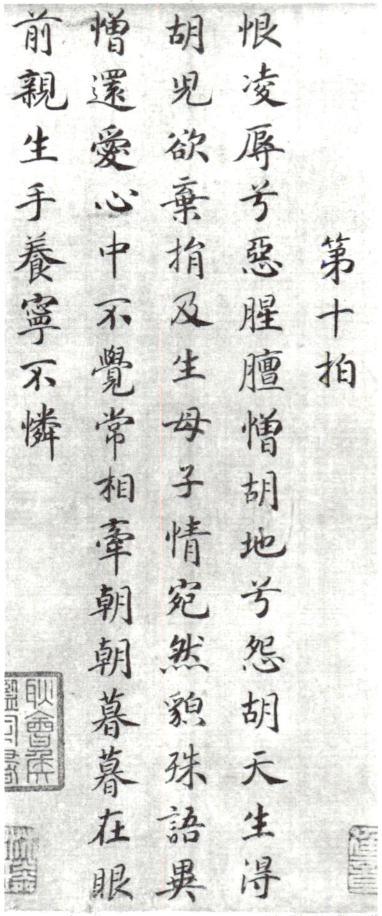

第十拍

恨凌辱兮惡腥膻憎胡地兮怨胡天生得
胡兒欲棄捐及生母子情宛然貌殊語異
憎還愛心中不覺常相牽朝朝暮暮在眼
前親生手養寧不憐

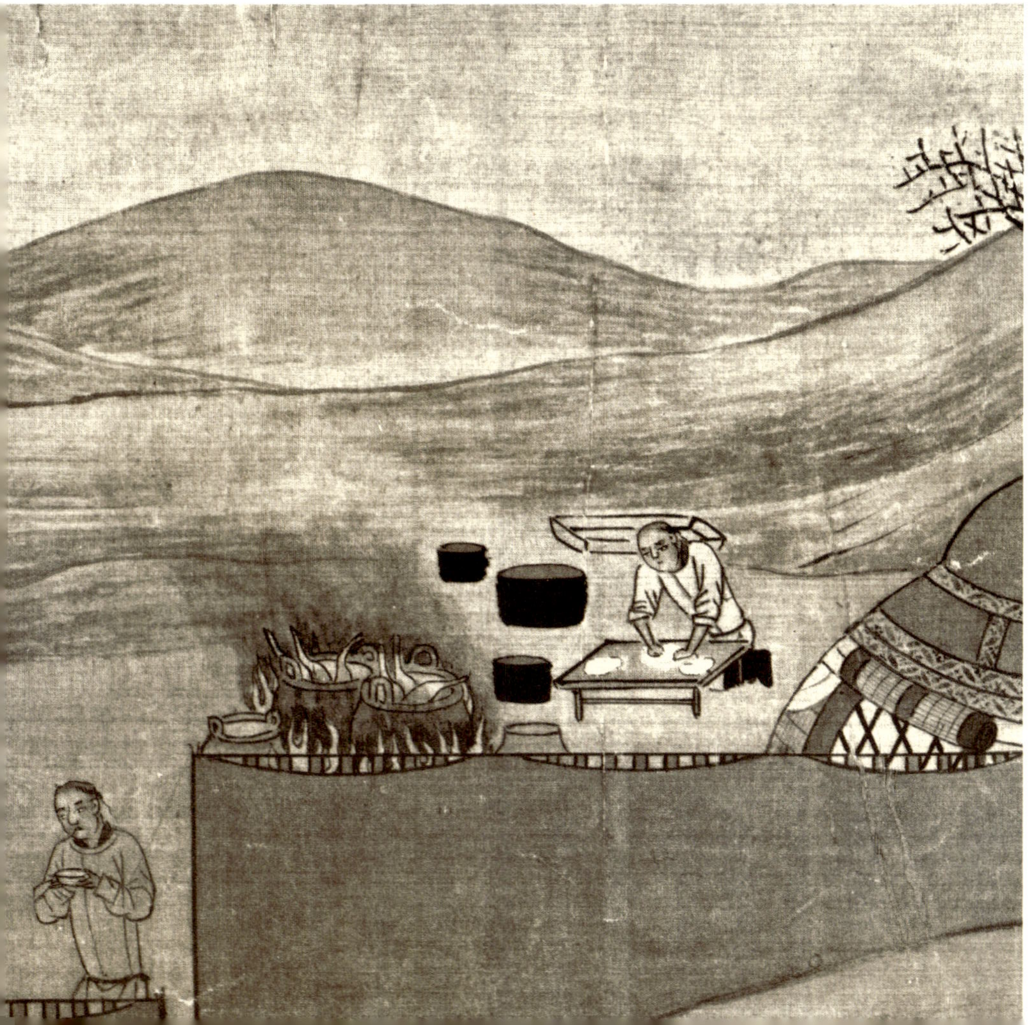

The father watches, sitting outside the yurt, while Wen-chi holds their child. Tribesmen approach to congratulate the couple. Beyond the screens the routines continue—the cook no doubt producing more of the smells mentioned in the poem. Behind the prince's yurt stands the splendid red-lacquered camel cart that Wen-chi rides in, its floor padded and matted, its sides walled with fabric. Its high, thin wheels make it an excellent crosser of sand, mud, and streams.

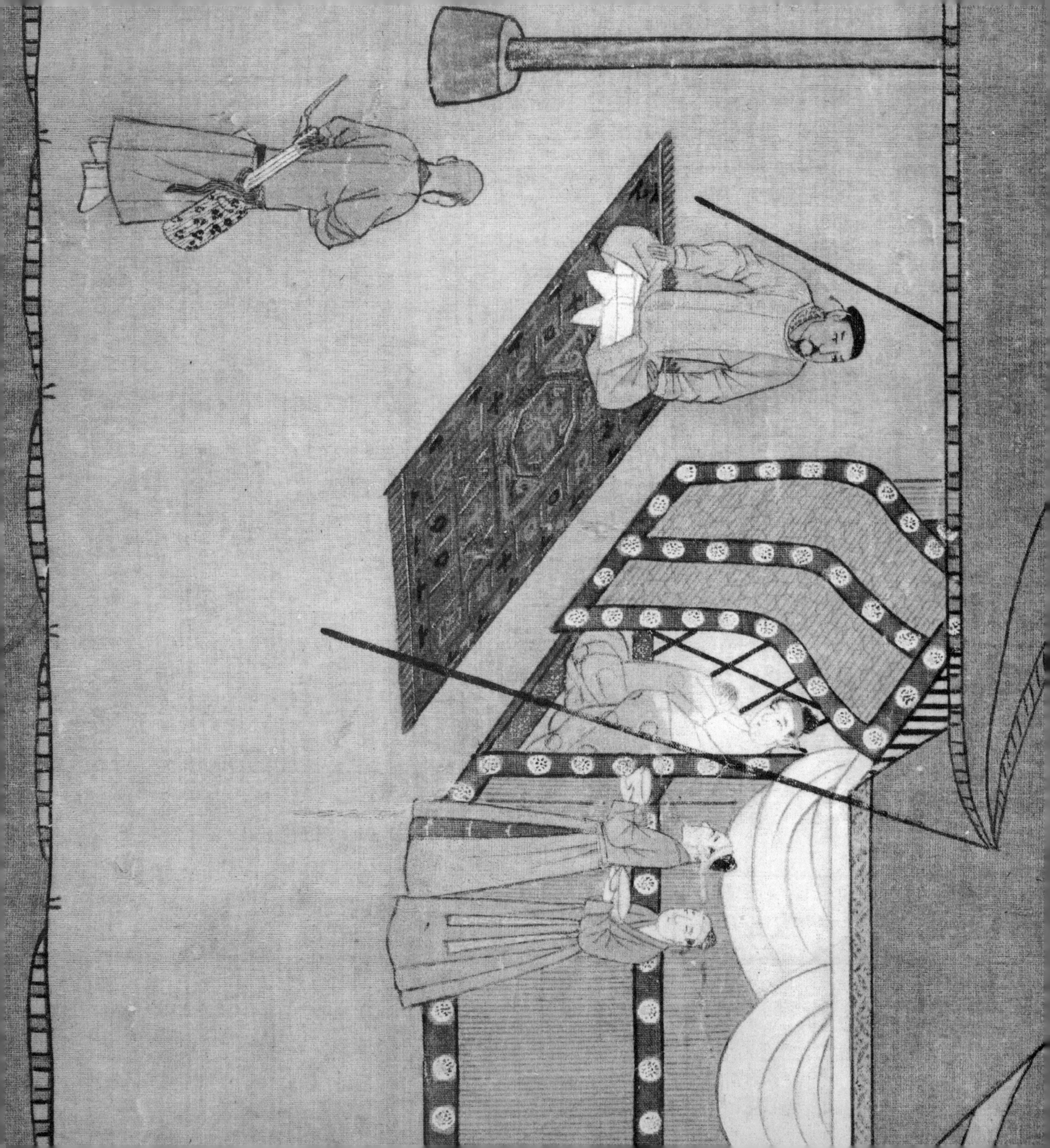

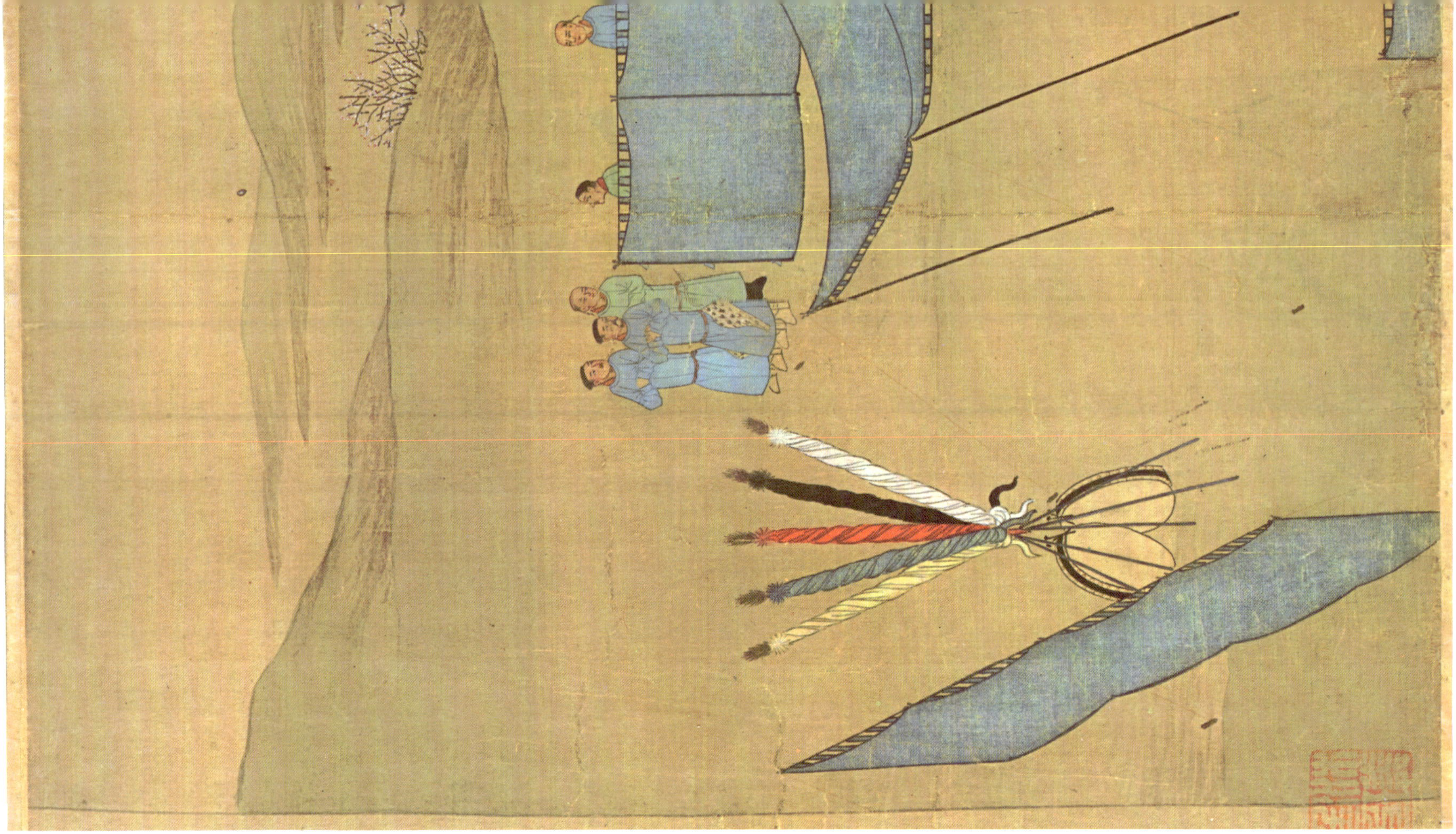

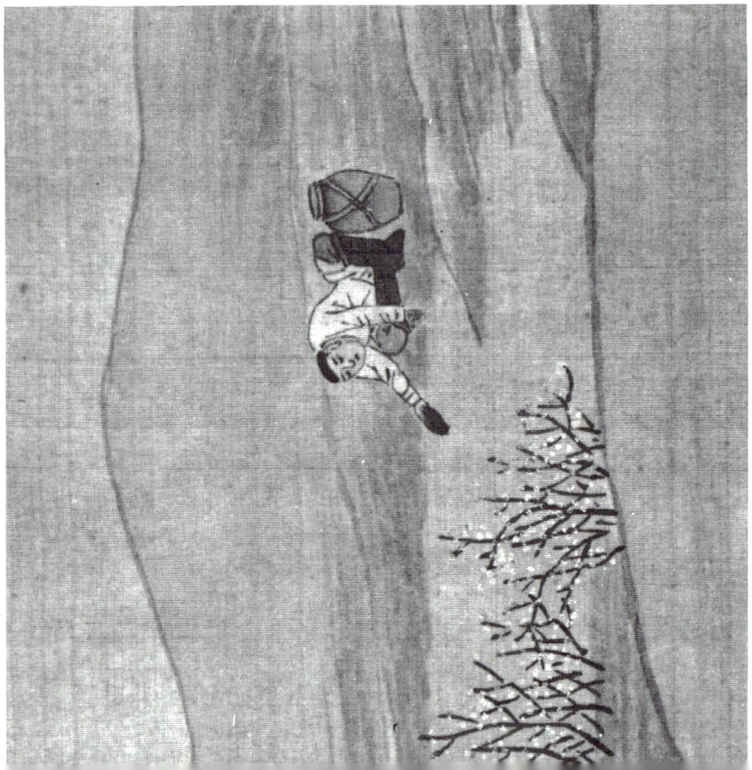

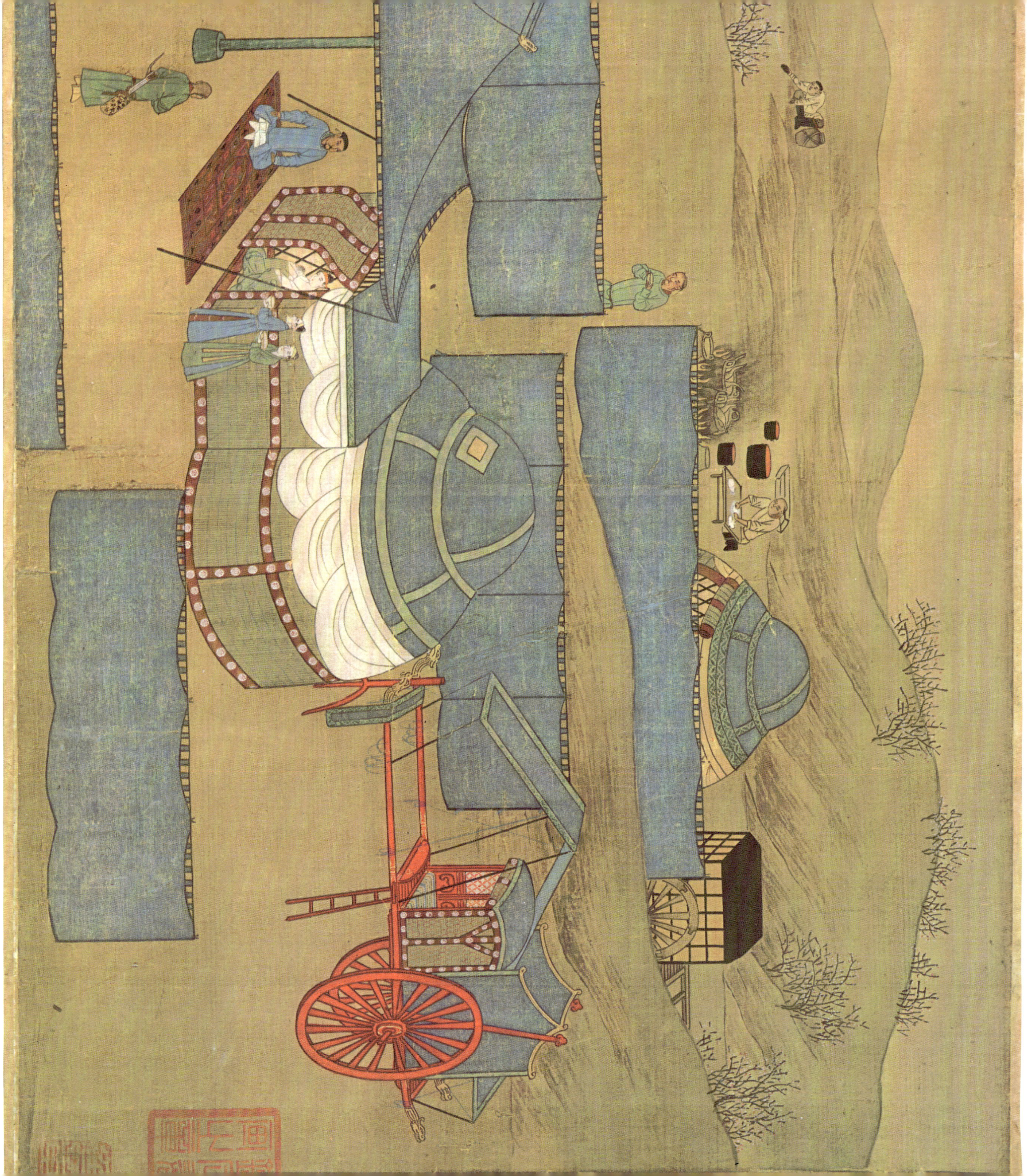

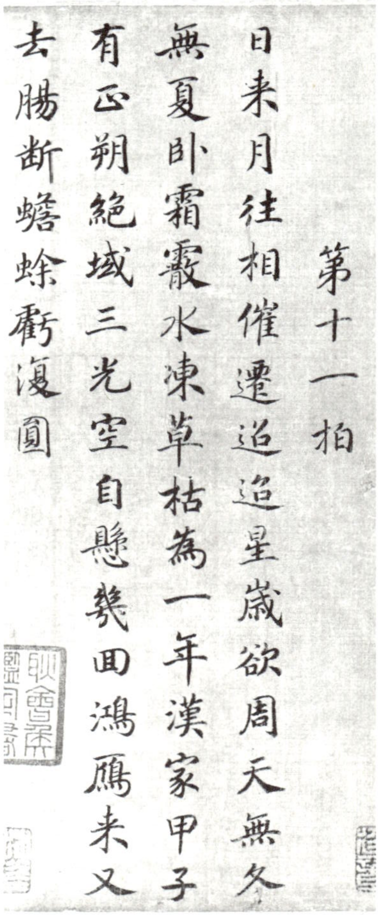

11 Watching Geese Fly South

Days come and months go by, time hurries along;
By the movement of the year-star, it is now almost twelve years.*
Winter or summer, we lie in frost and sleet;
When the water freezes and the grass withers I mark another year.
In China we have a cyclical calendar to mark the full and new moon,
But in these far-off lands the sun, moon, and stars only hang meaninglessly in the sky.
Many times the migratory geese come and go;
I am brokenhearted as the moon wanes and again grows full.

* Jupiter.

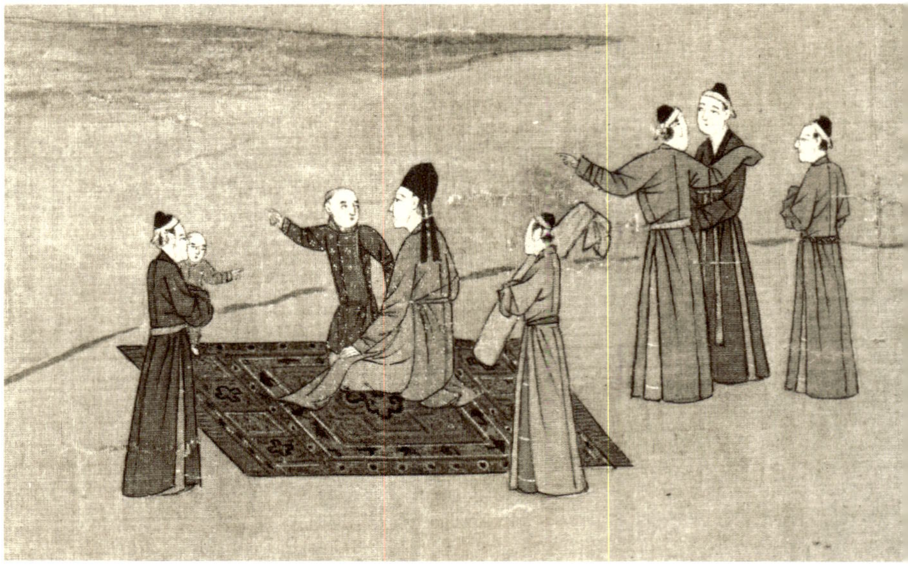

Wen-chi now has two children. Autumn foliage is again on the trees. A ribbon of geese crosses the sky, winging south. While the Chinese habitually keep track of the seasons and years, so that lives of people and affairs of state may be properly ordered in accord with the workings of the universe, Wen-chi, as an exile, sees seasonal change only as part of an interminable flux of time.

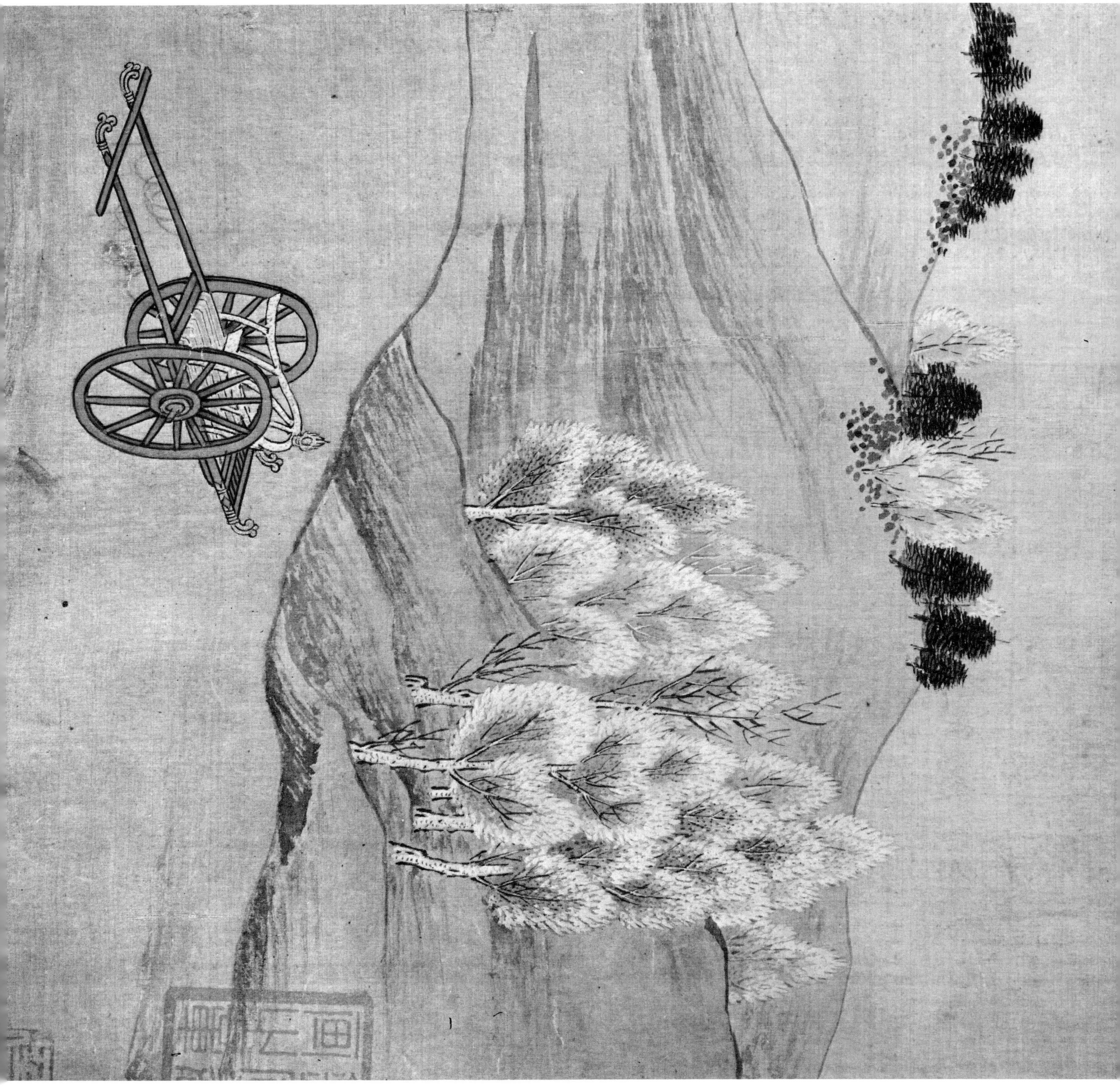

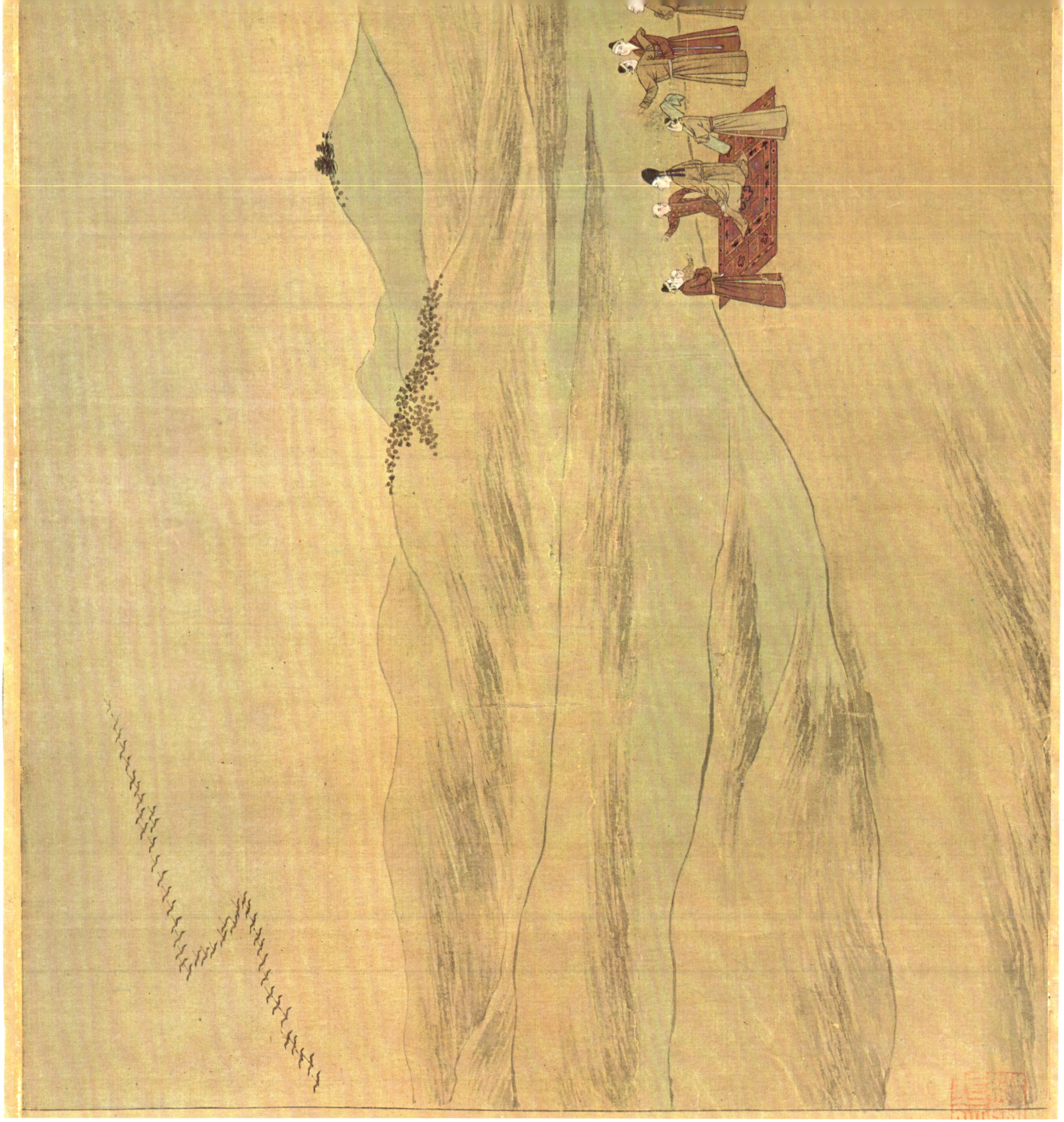

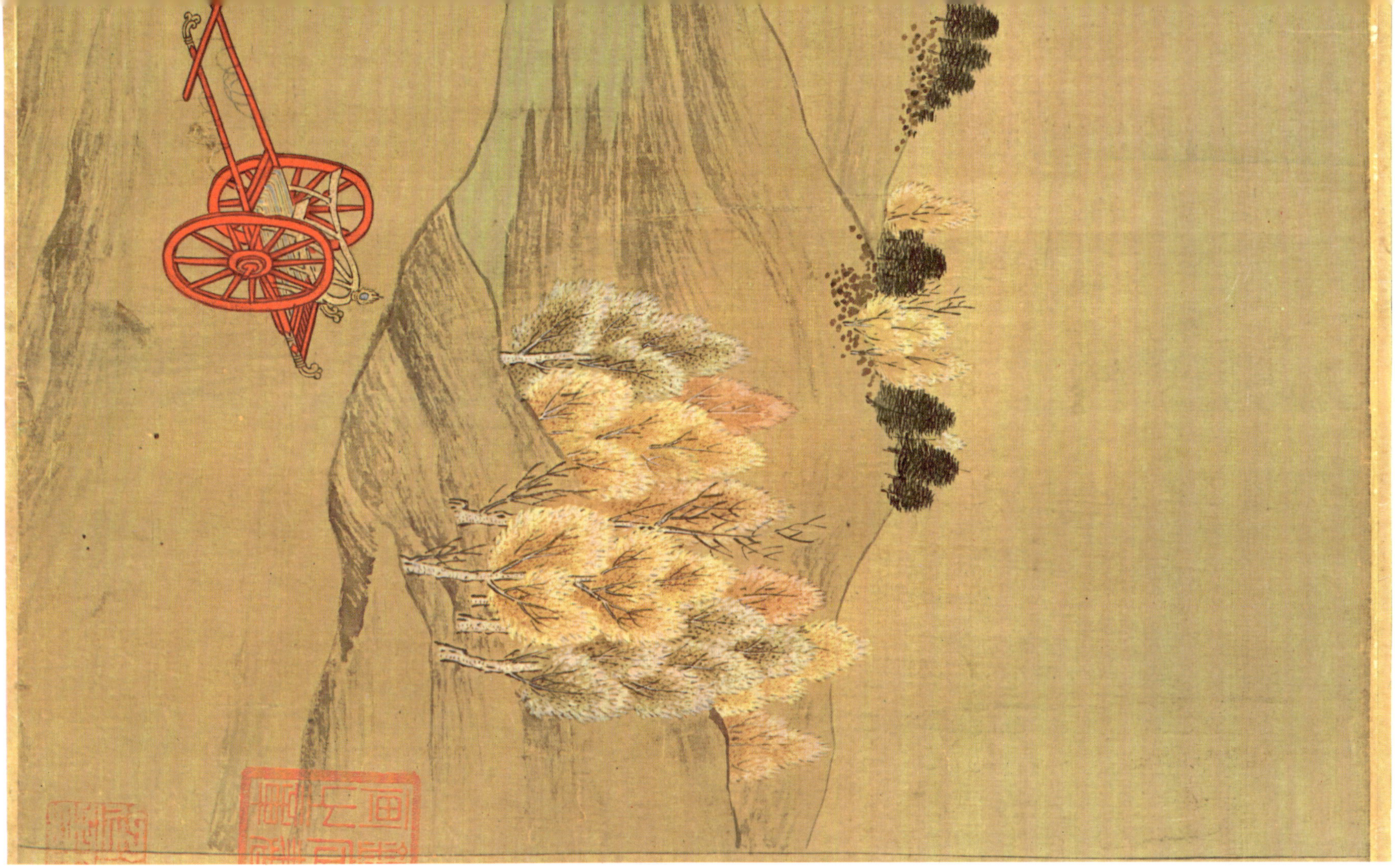

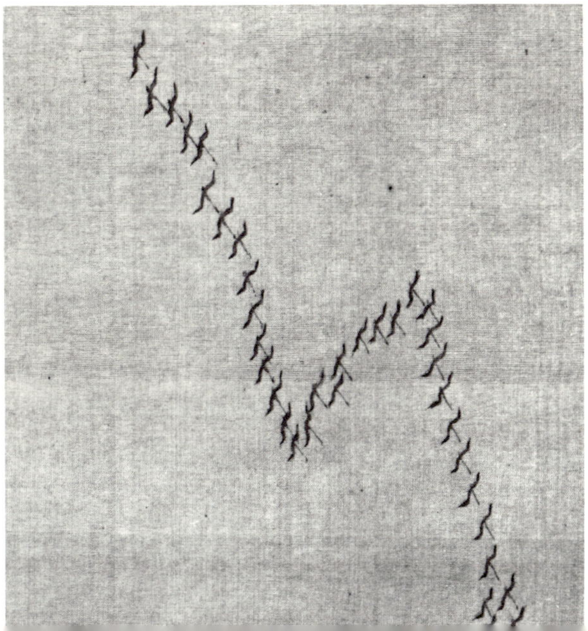

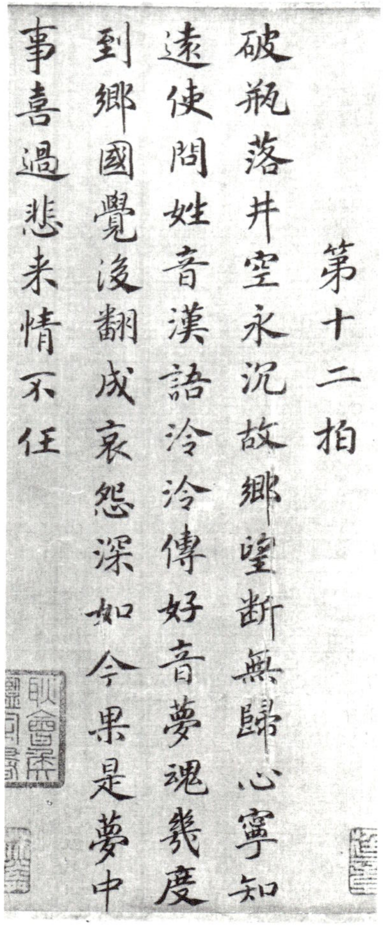

12 Messengers Arrive

A broken bottle dropped into a well is lost forever.
With no hope in sight, I have given up all thought of returning.
How could I have known that an envoy would come from afar, asking names?
The Han speech, pleasing to the ear, brings happy news.
How many times had my soul wandered home in my dreams?
Each time after I awoke my sorrow was deeper still.
Now that I am faced with what I dreamt,
Grief comes after joy; my emotions become unbearable.

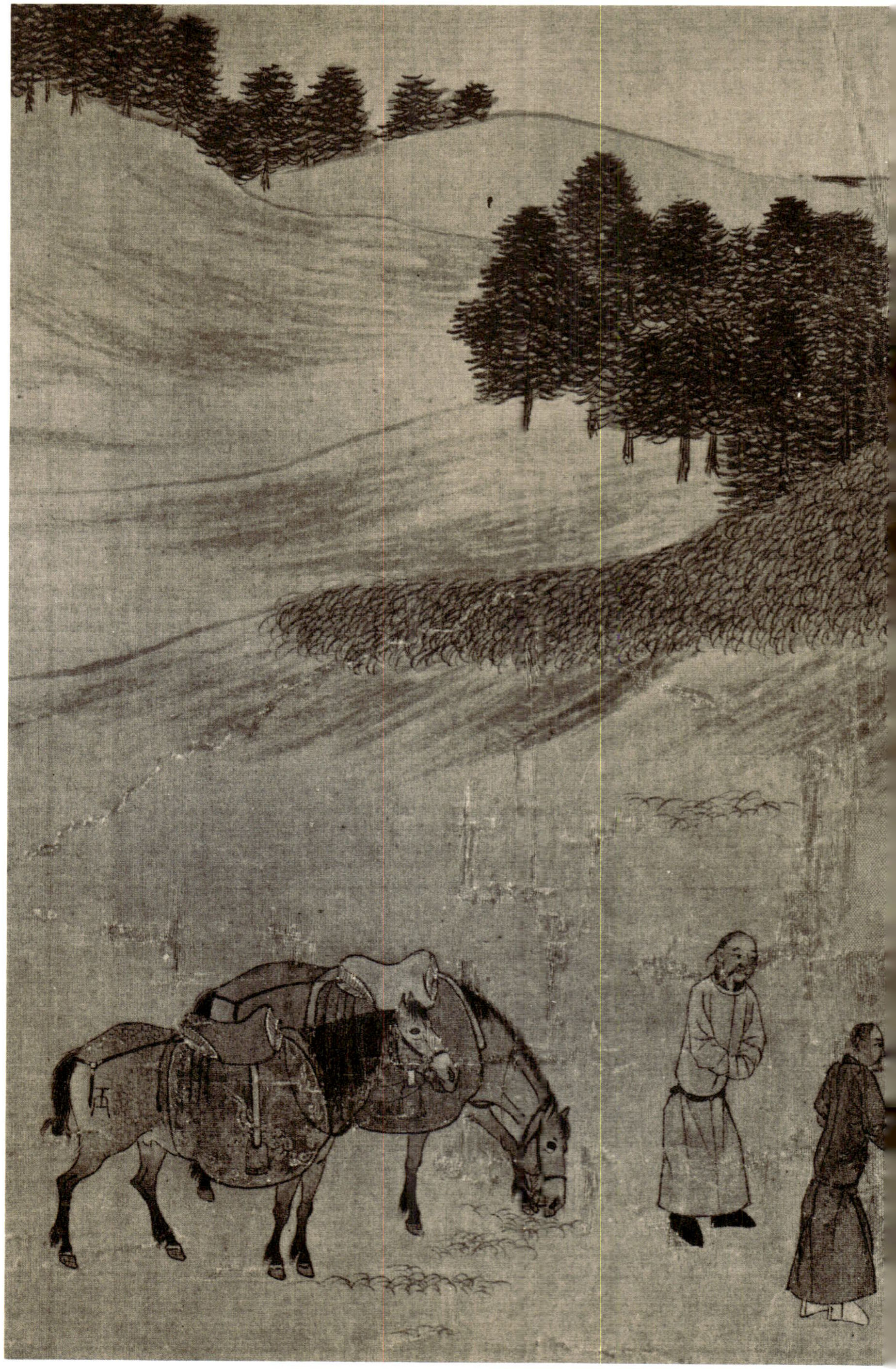

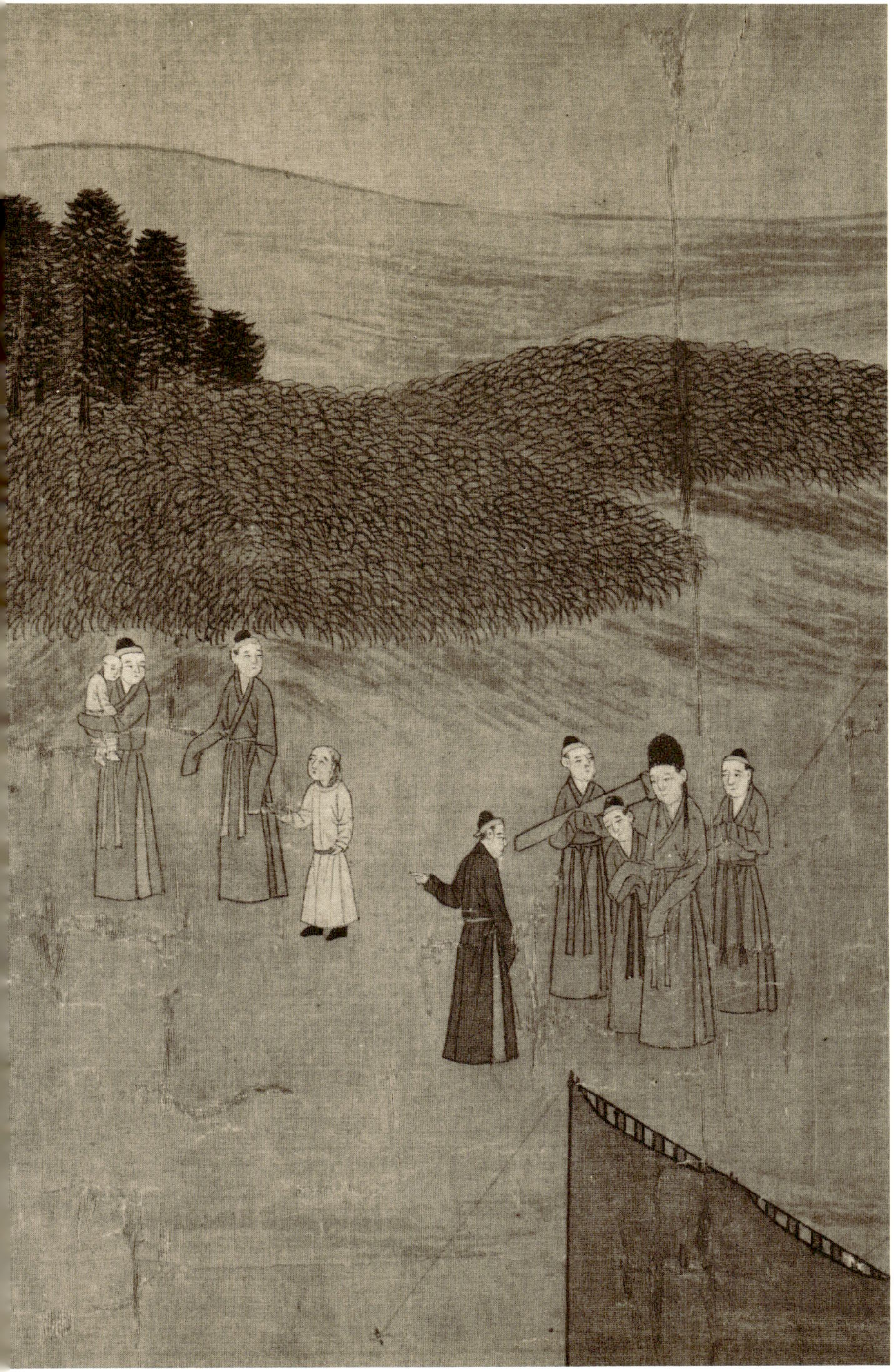

Summer green is on the hills when messengers sent by the Chinese approach with word of the impending ransom. Wen-chi's first reactions of surprise and joy are followed immediately by a new kind of grief as the implication of her return to China—permanent separation from her husband and children—strikes her.

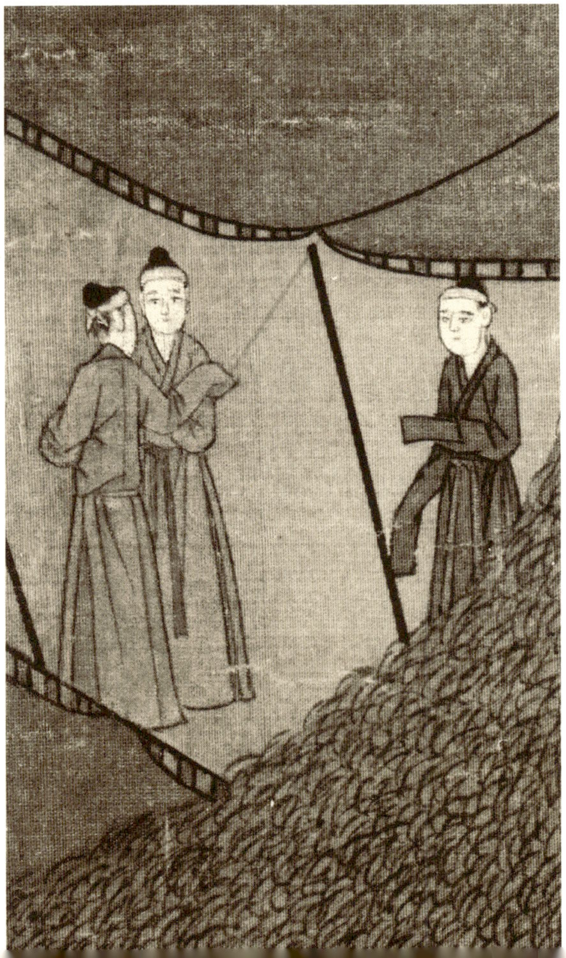

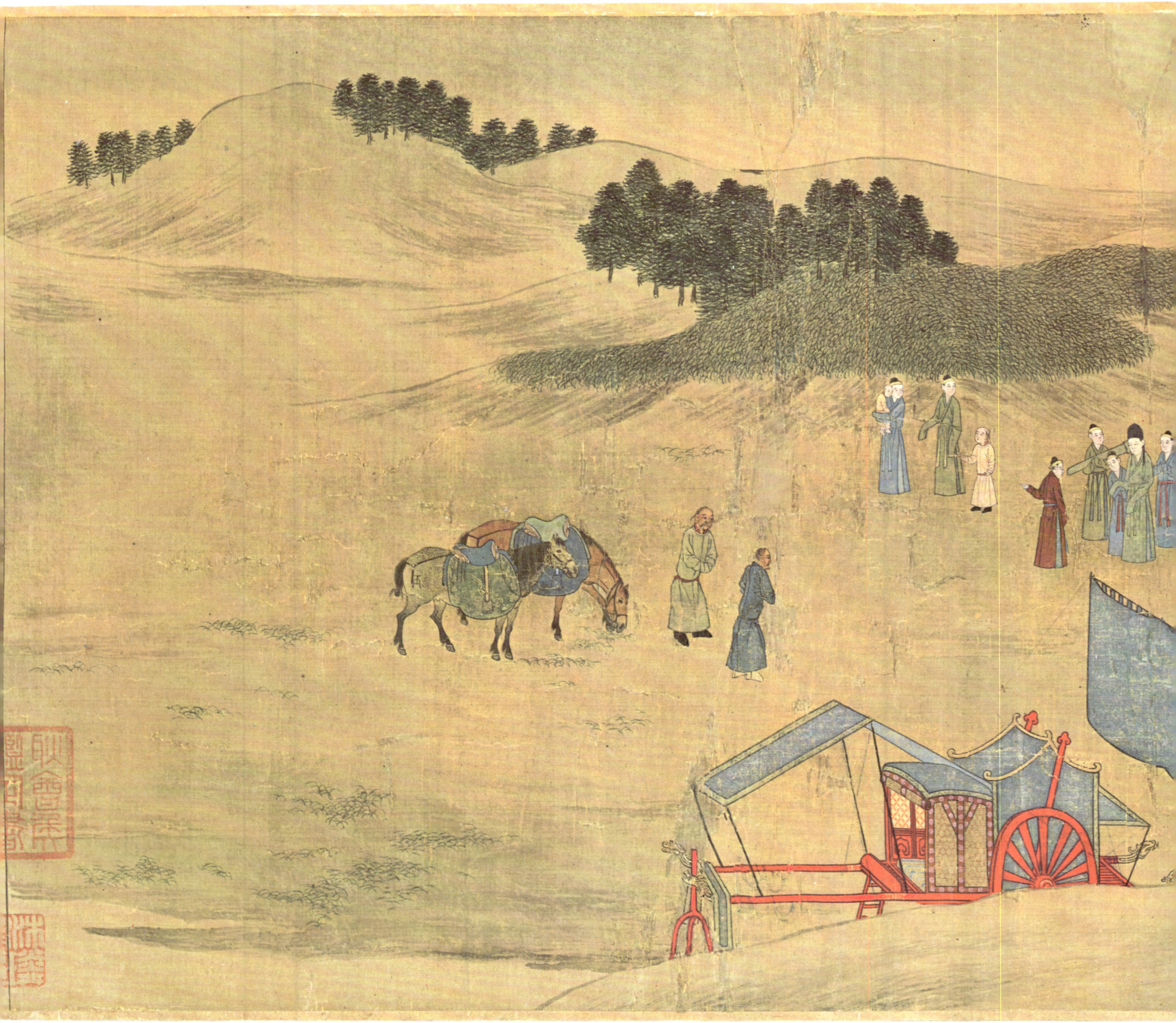

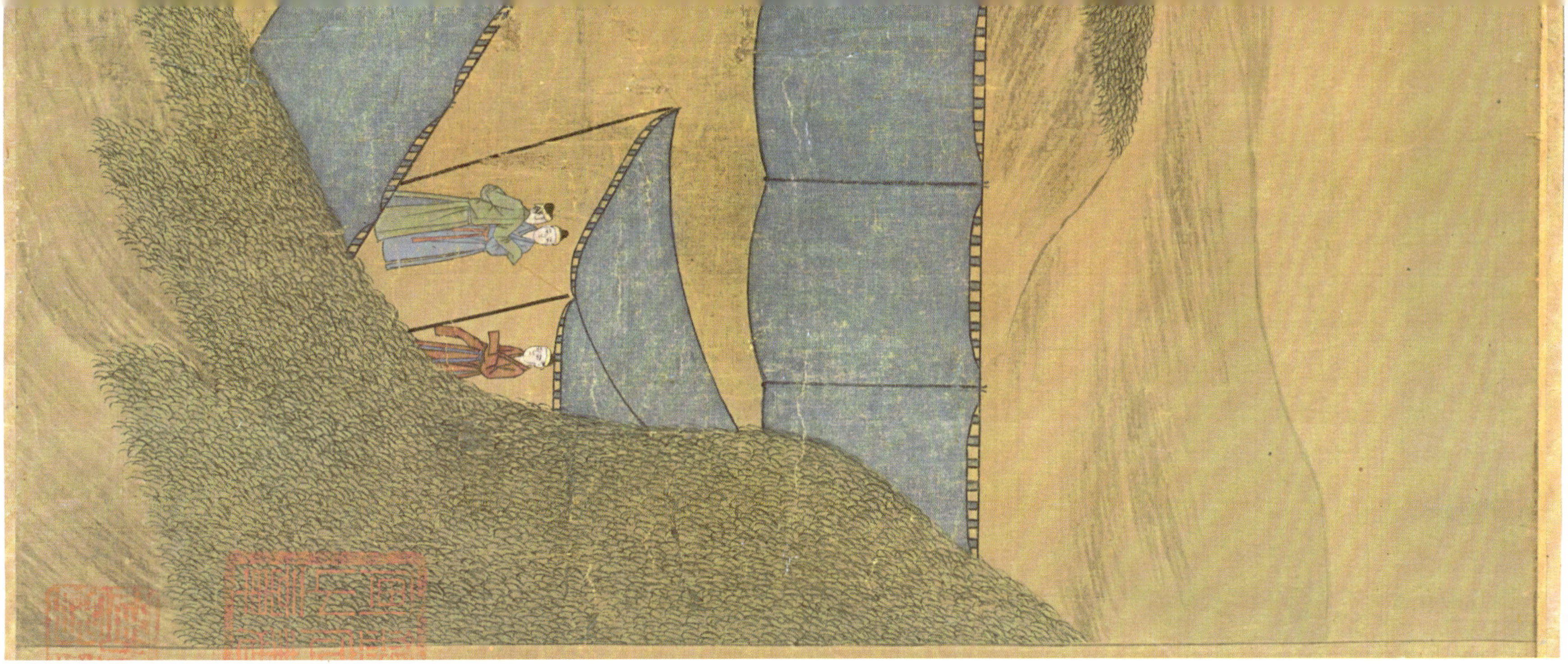

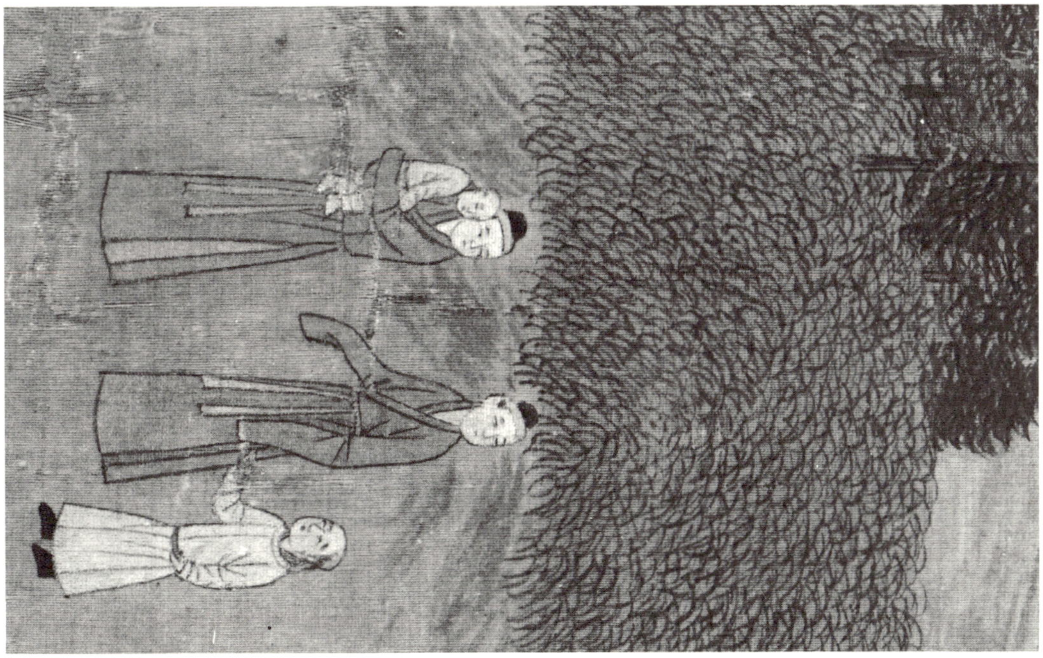

13 The Farewell

My children pull at my clothes, one on either side;
I cannot take them with me, but in leaving them behind, how I shall miss them!
To return home and to depart in sorrow—my emotions are mixed.
Now I must abandon my children in order to return home.
Across ten thousand miles of mountains and rivers, I shall arrive at our border stations.
Once having turned away, forever there shall be no news from my children.
With tear-stained face I turn toward the setting sun;
All day long I have stood there, looking to the south and then to the north.

The story approaches its climax. The cooks make last preparations in their screened-off area, the wine servers stand ready, the tall red serving table is in place, and cushions and tables are formally set for the banquet no one will eat with relish. Many in the camp, men as well as women, are overcome. The prince lifts his sleeves to blot his tears. His older son tugs at Wen-chi's garments while the younger boy, crying, reaches from the arms of a nurse. The prince's horses, their tails hanging long, are saddled. The bearer of his parasol stands ready. Beyond the camel cart, indifferent to the drama, a tribesman stretches and yawns. At a respectful distance, behind a hill, the Chinese envoy and his retinue wait beneath the imperial banner.

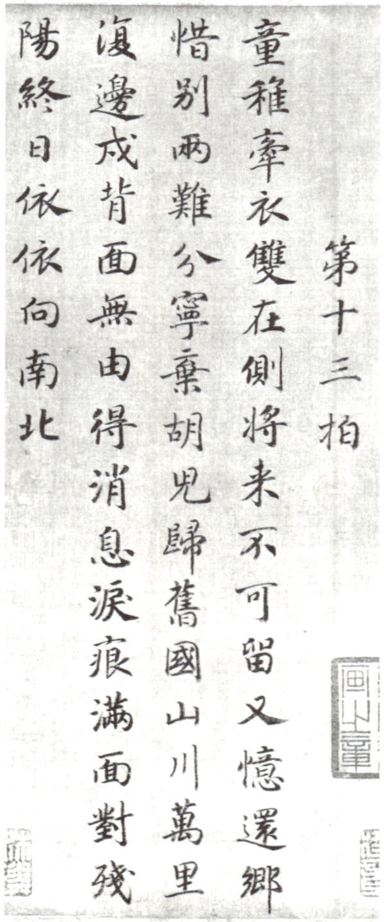

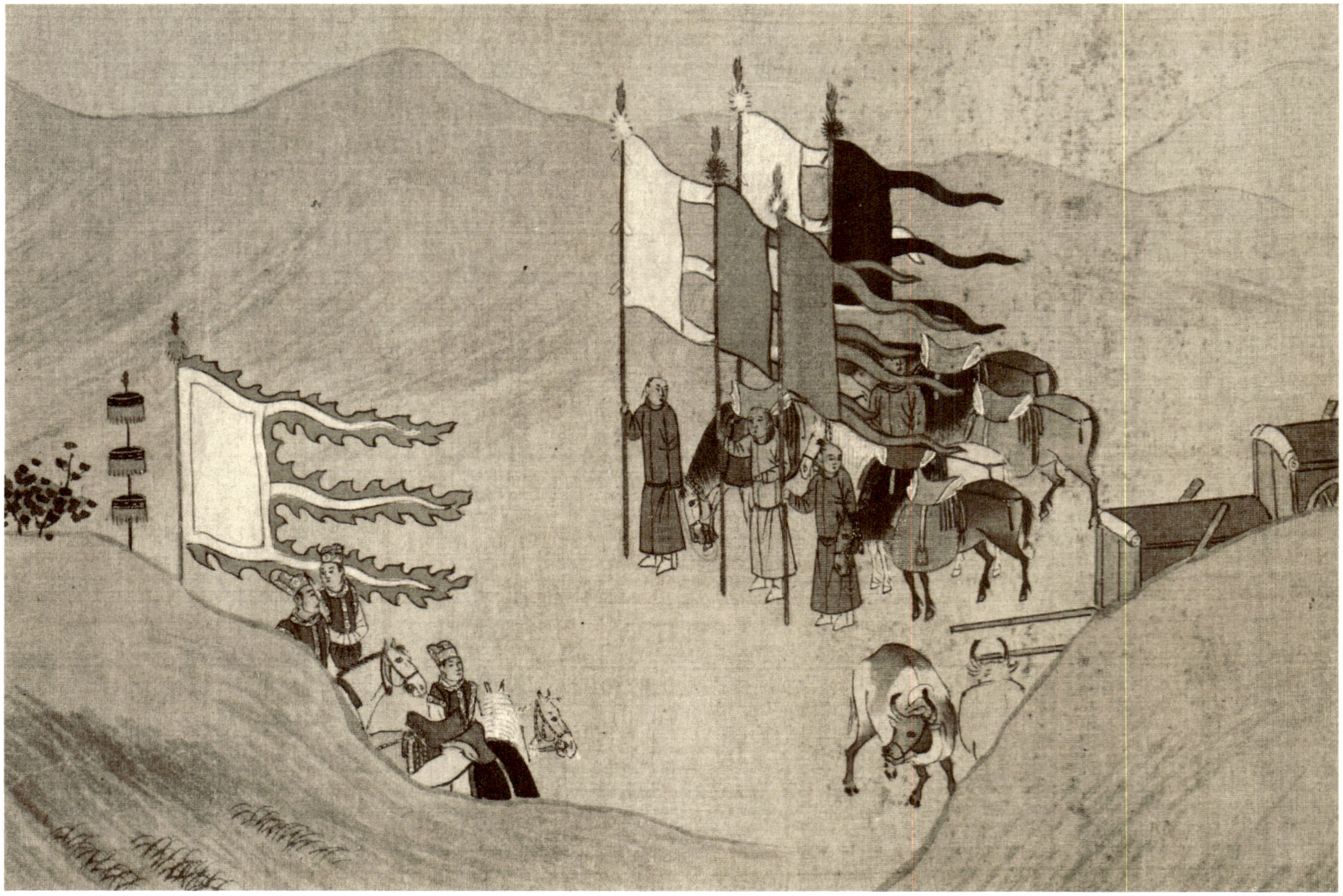

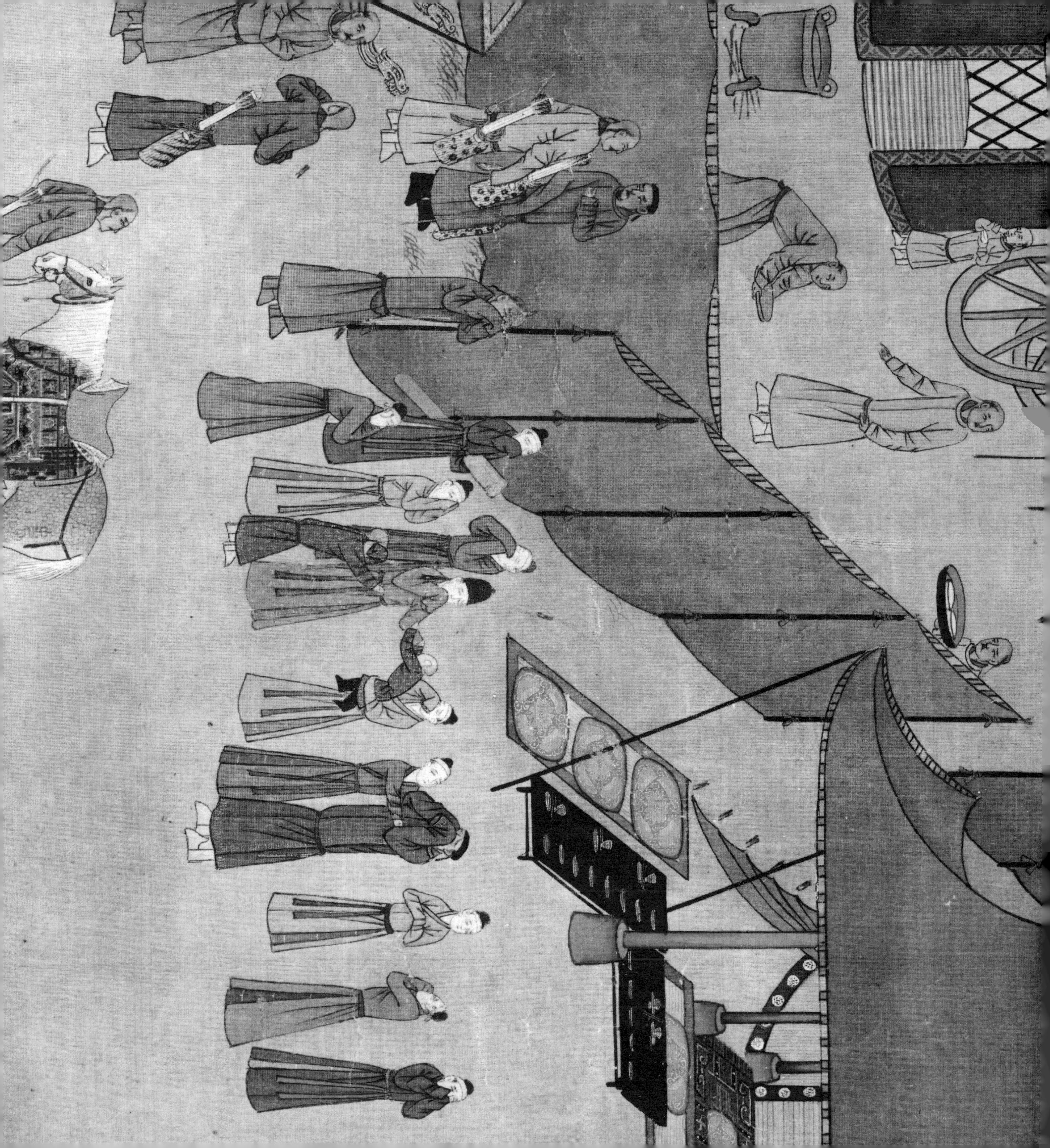

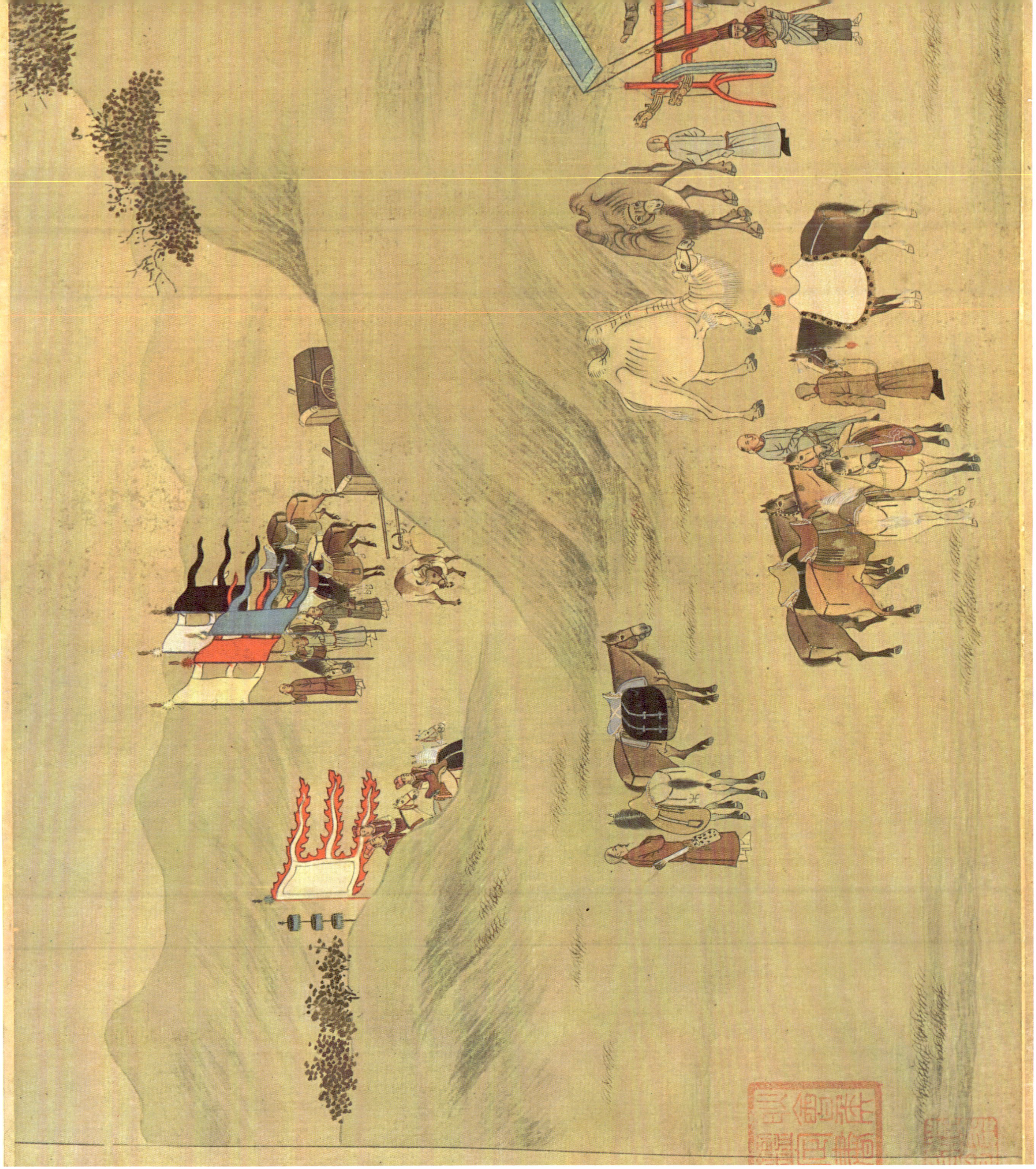

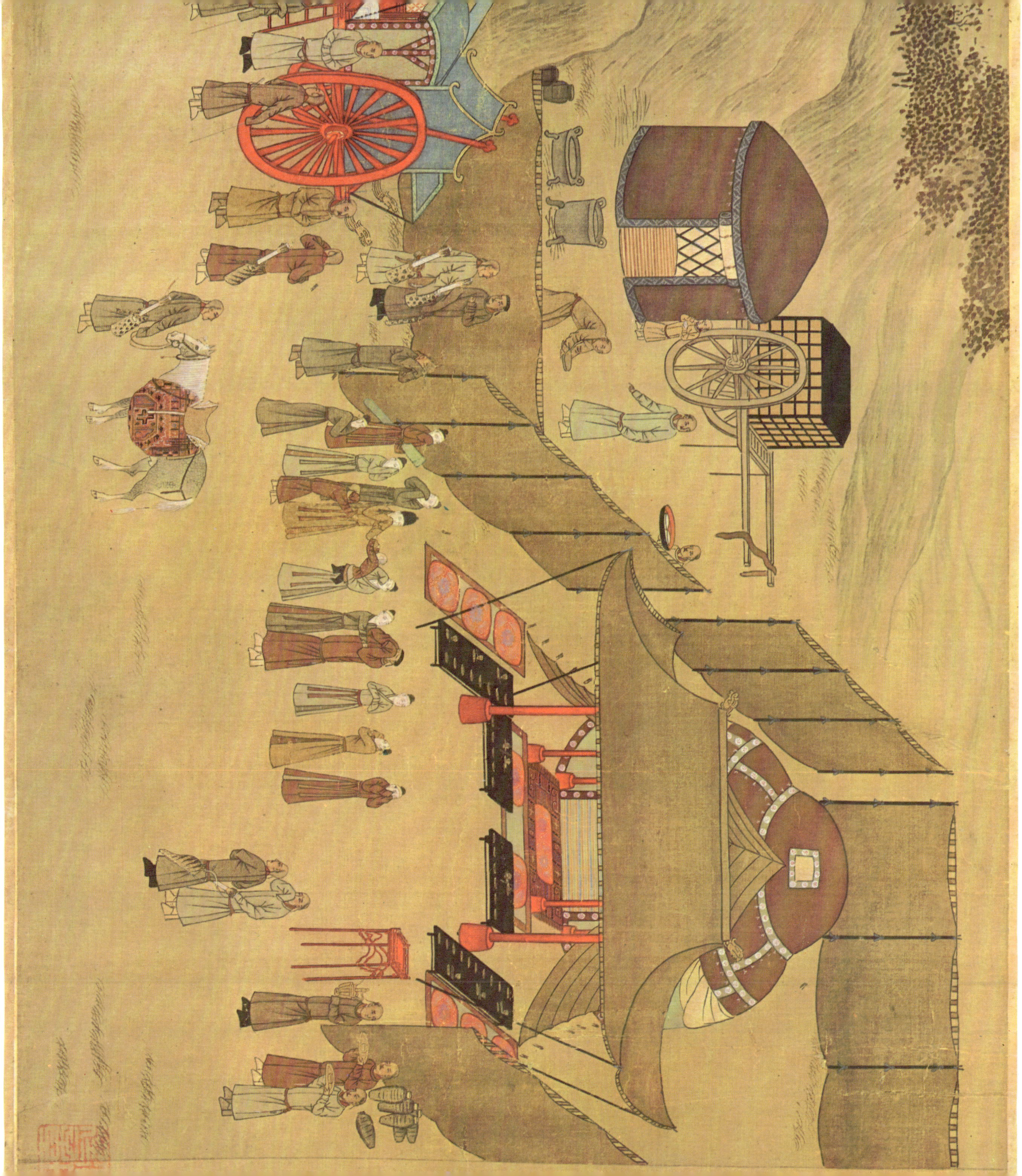

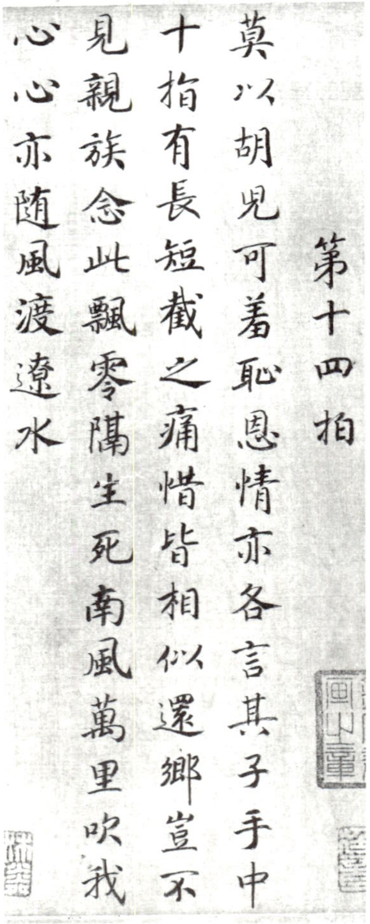

第十四拍
莫以胡兒可著恥恩情亦各言其子手中
十指有長短截之痛惜皆相似還鄉豈不
見親族念此飄零隔生死南風萬里吹我
心心亦隨風渡遼水

14 The Return Journey Begins

Do not think that the nomad children cause me shame;
Anyone would speak of his or her children with love.
The ten fingers of the two hands are of different lengths,
Yet the pain of one cut off is the same as for any other.
Upon my return, I shall be reunited with my kinsmen,
Then this part of my life will be as remote as the dead are from the living.
The southern wind blows across ten thousand miles to stir my heart;
*My heart will follow the wind and cross the Liao River.**

*In modern Jehol and Liao-ning provinces.

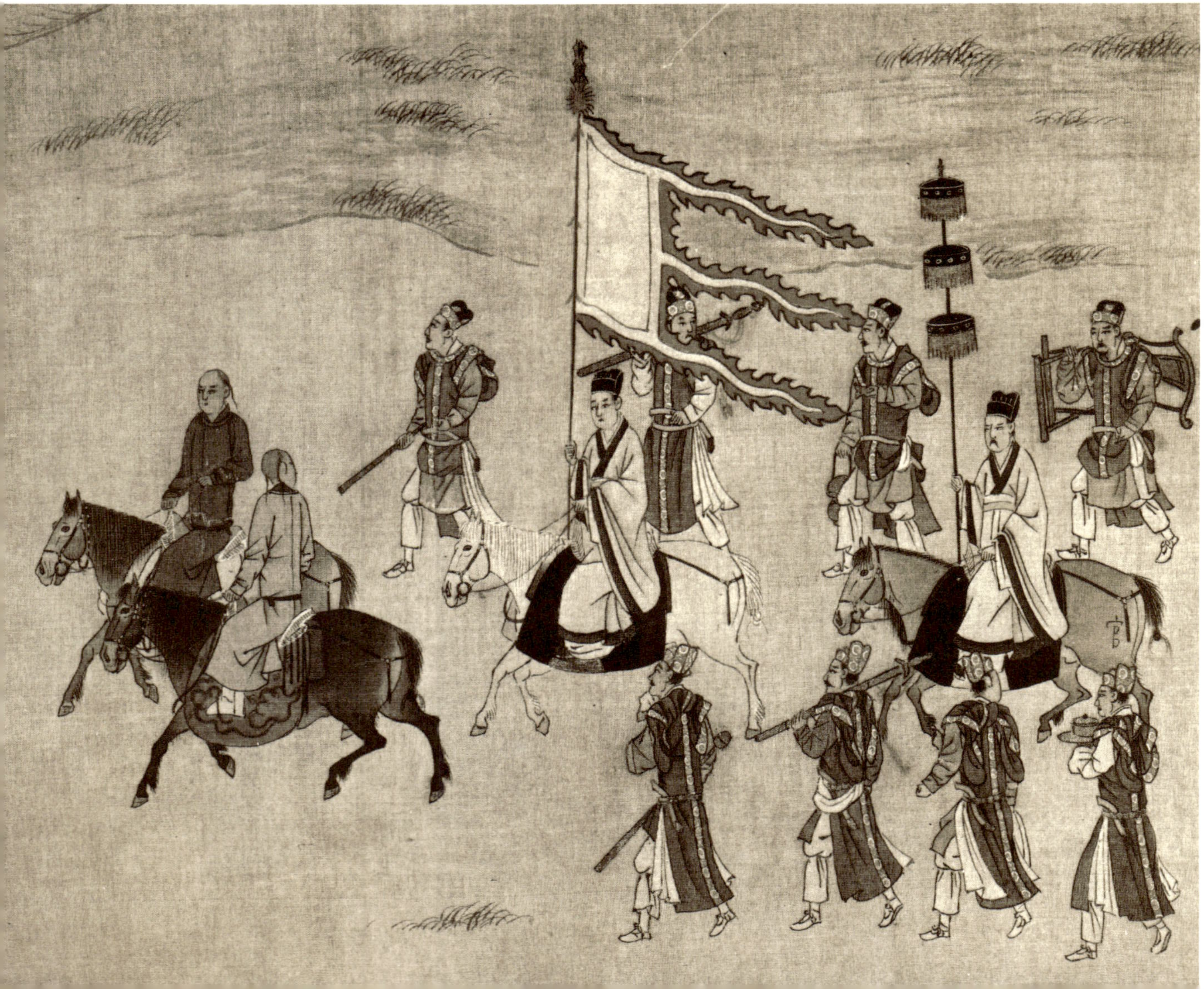

Preceded by nomad outriders and sword-carrying Chinese, the Chinese envoy and the nomad prince ride side by side. Since the journey will be long, the pace is moderate: the footman carrying the envoy's folding chair has no trouble keeping up. The procession stretches far back into the hills even as the leaders draw near a wave-filled river. Wen-chi travels concealed from view in her camel cart. Such a vehicle, covered with a blue fabric, is described in the *History of Liao* as proper for a Khitan princess (Introduction, note 11). The brand on the envoy's horse, pronounced *kuan,* means "official."

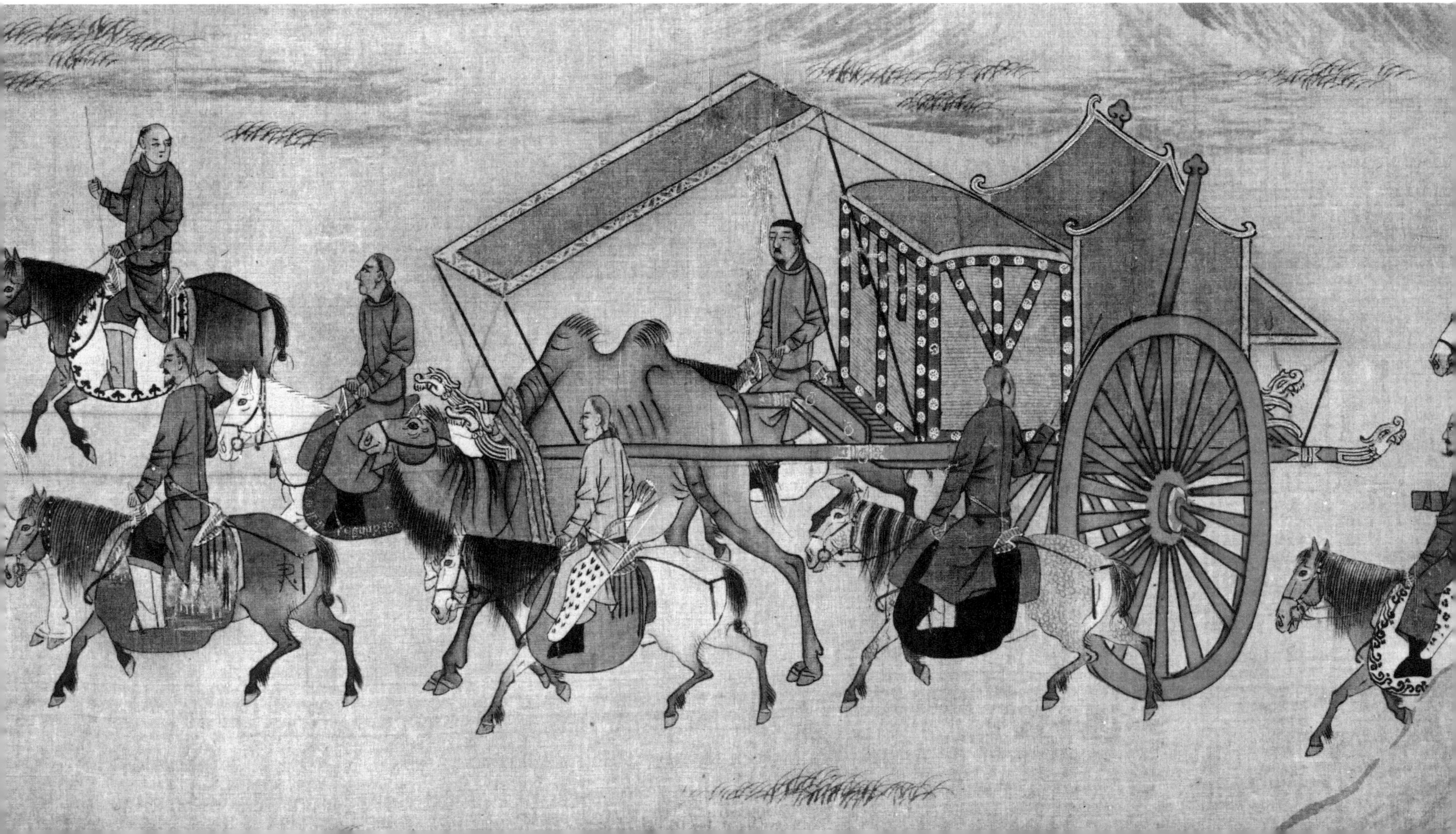

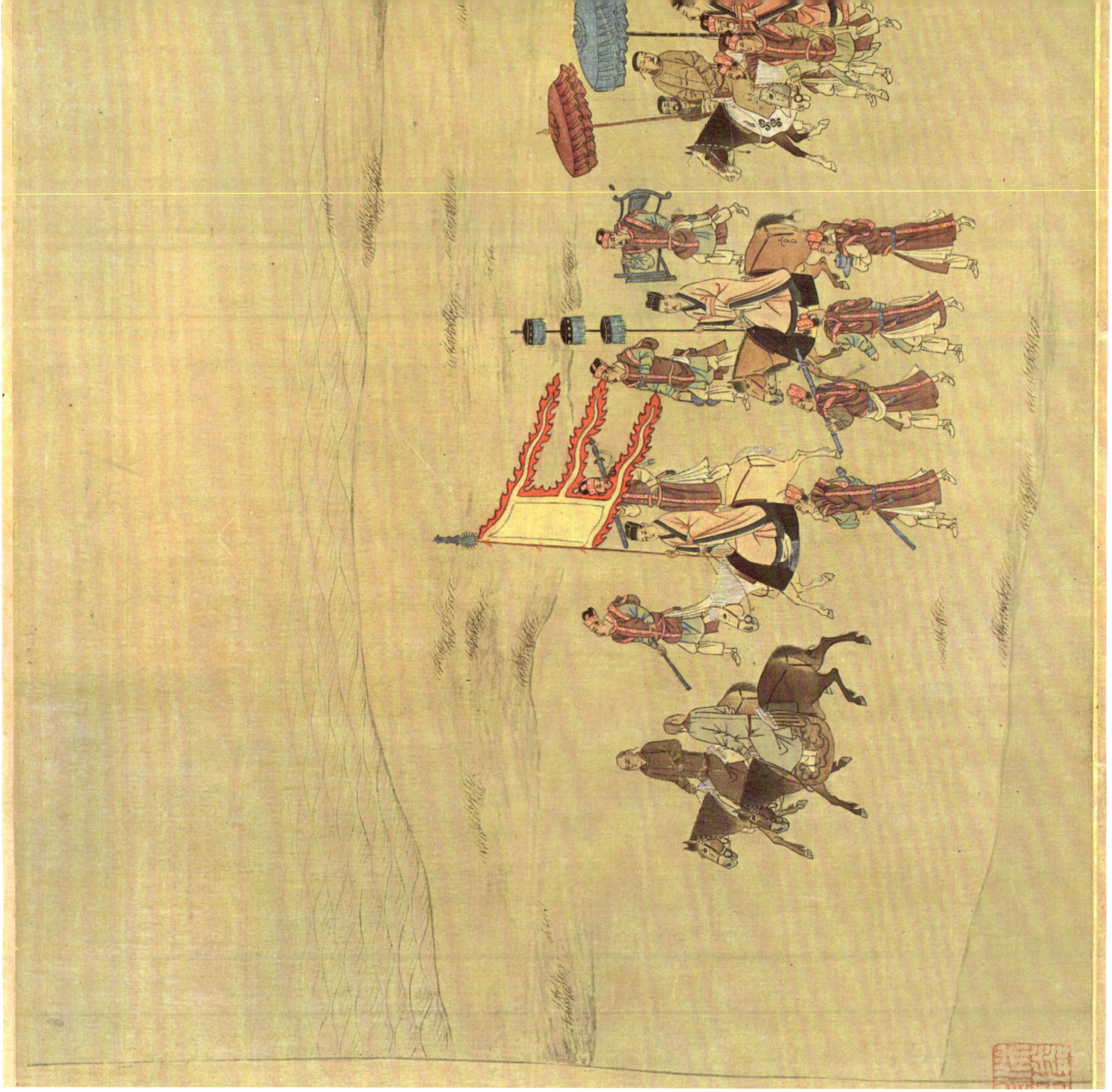

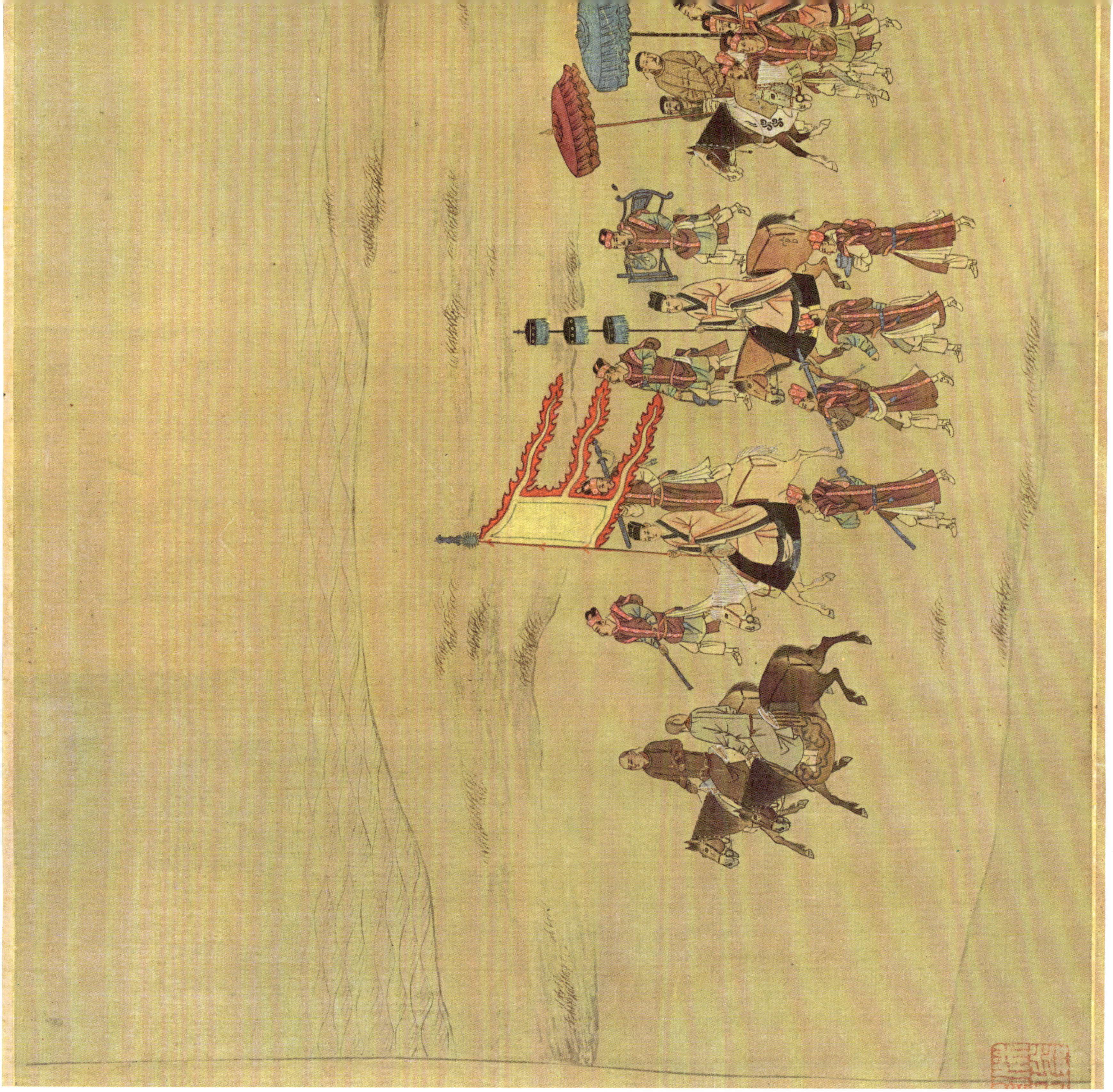

Preceded by nomad outriders and sword-carrying Chinese, the Chinese envoy and the nomad prince ride side by side. Since the journey will be long, the pace is moderate: the footman carrying the envoy's folding chair has no trouble keeping up. The procession stretches far back into the hills even as the leaders draw near a wave-filled river. Wen-chi travels concealed from view in her camel cart. Such a vehicle, covered with a blue fabric, is described in the *History of Liao* as proper for a Khitan princess (Introduction, note 11). The brand on the envoy's horse, pronounced *kuan*, means "official."

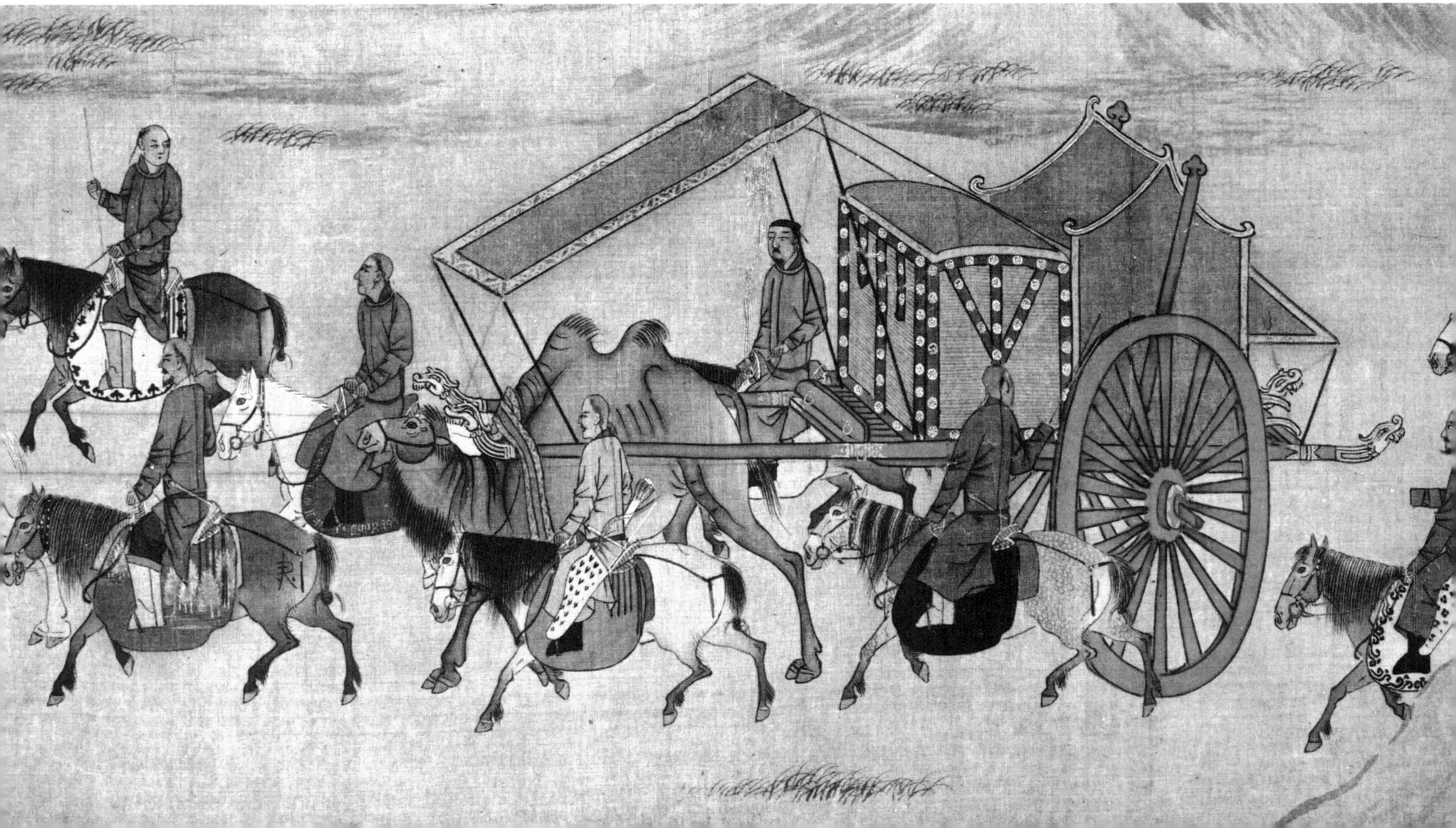

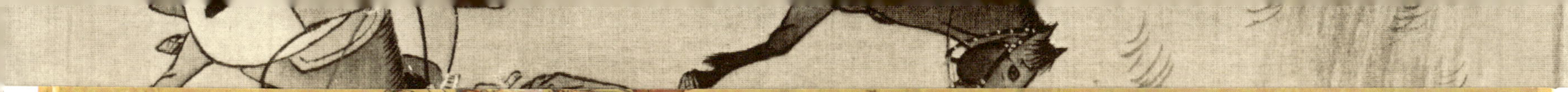

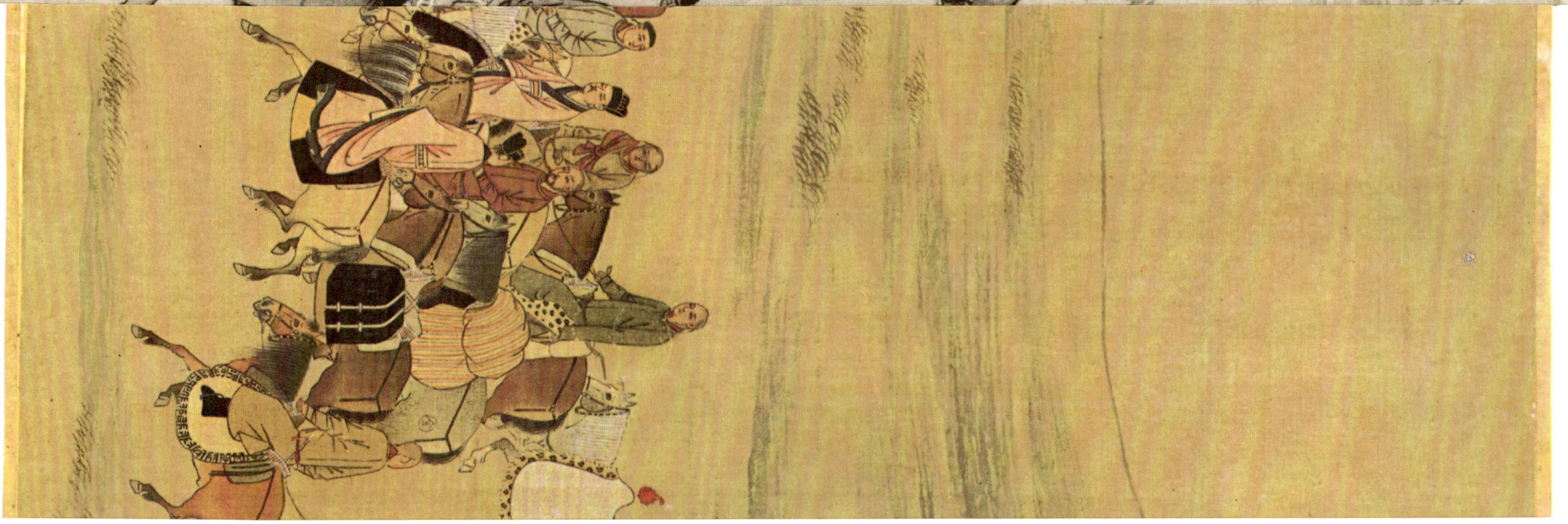

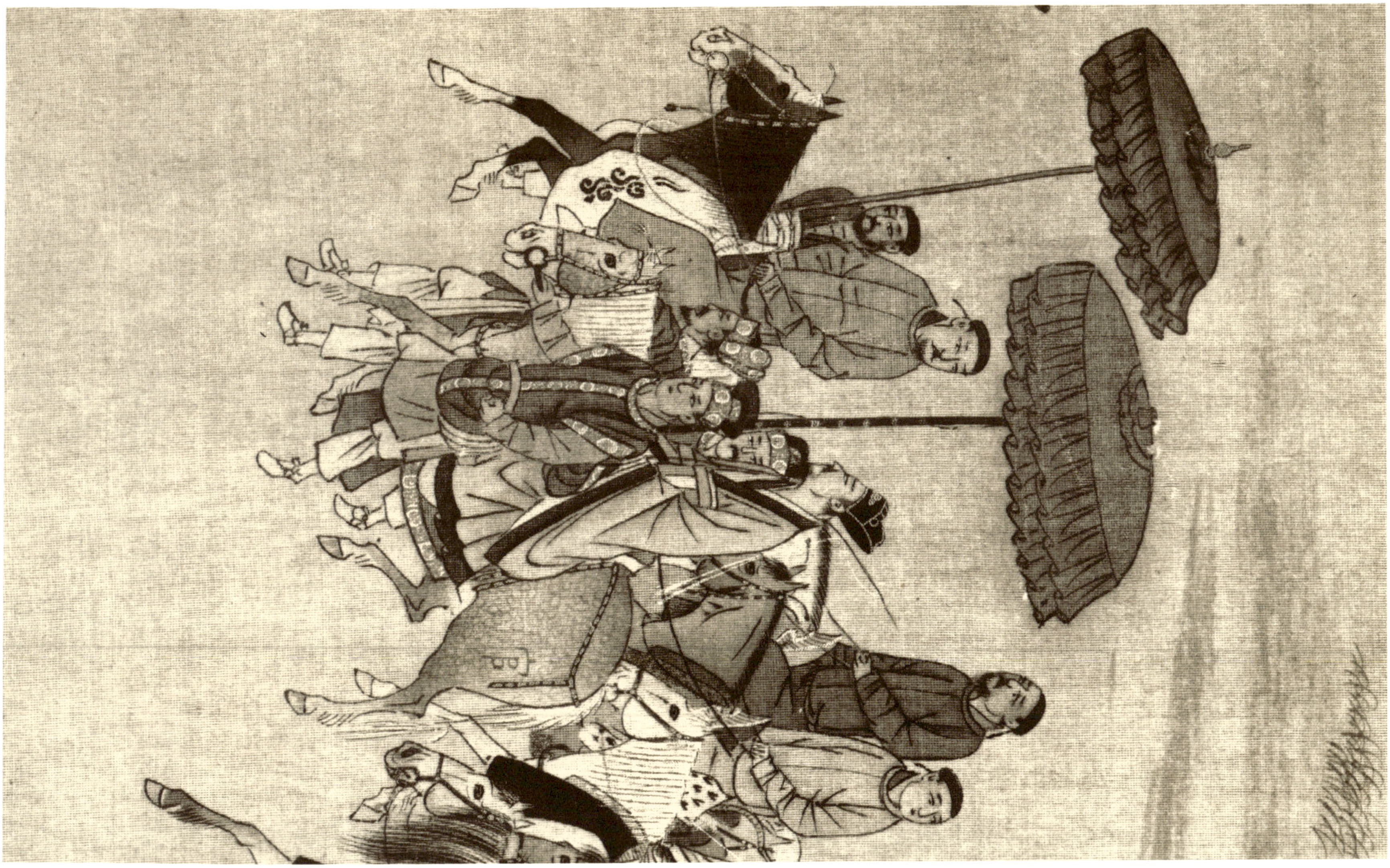

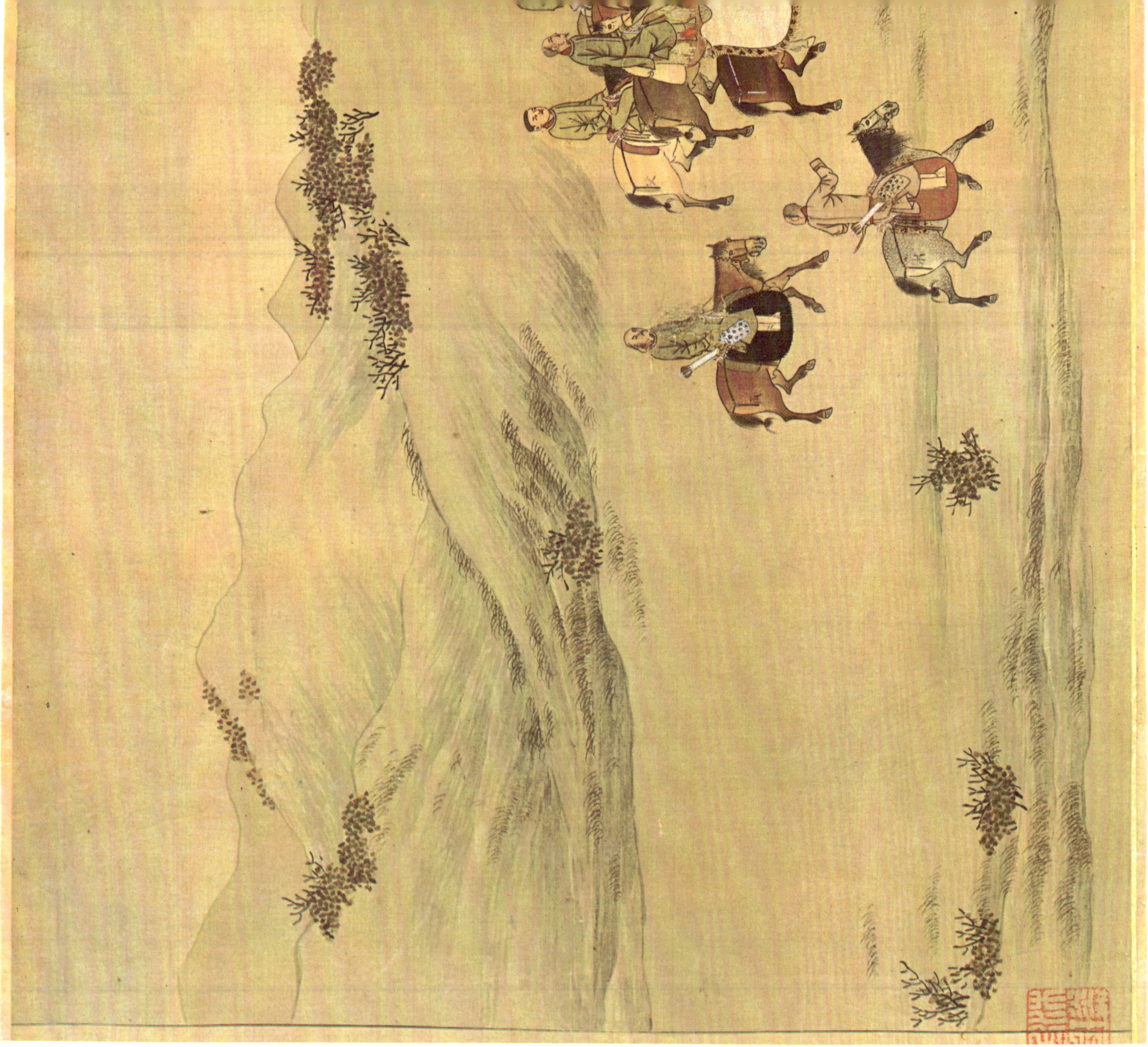

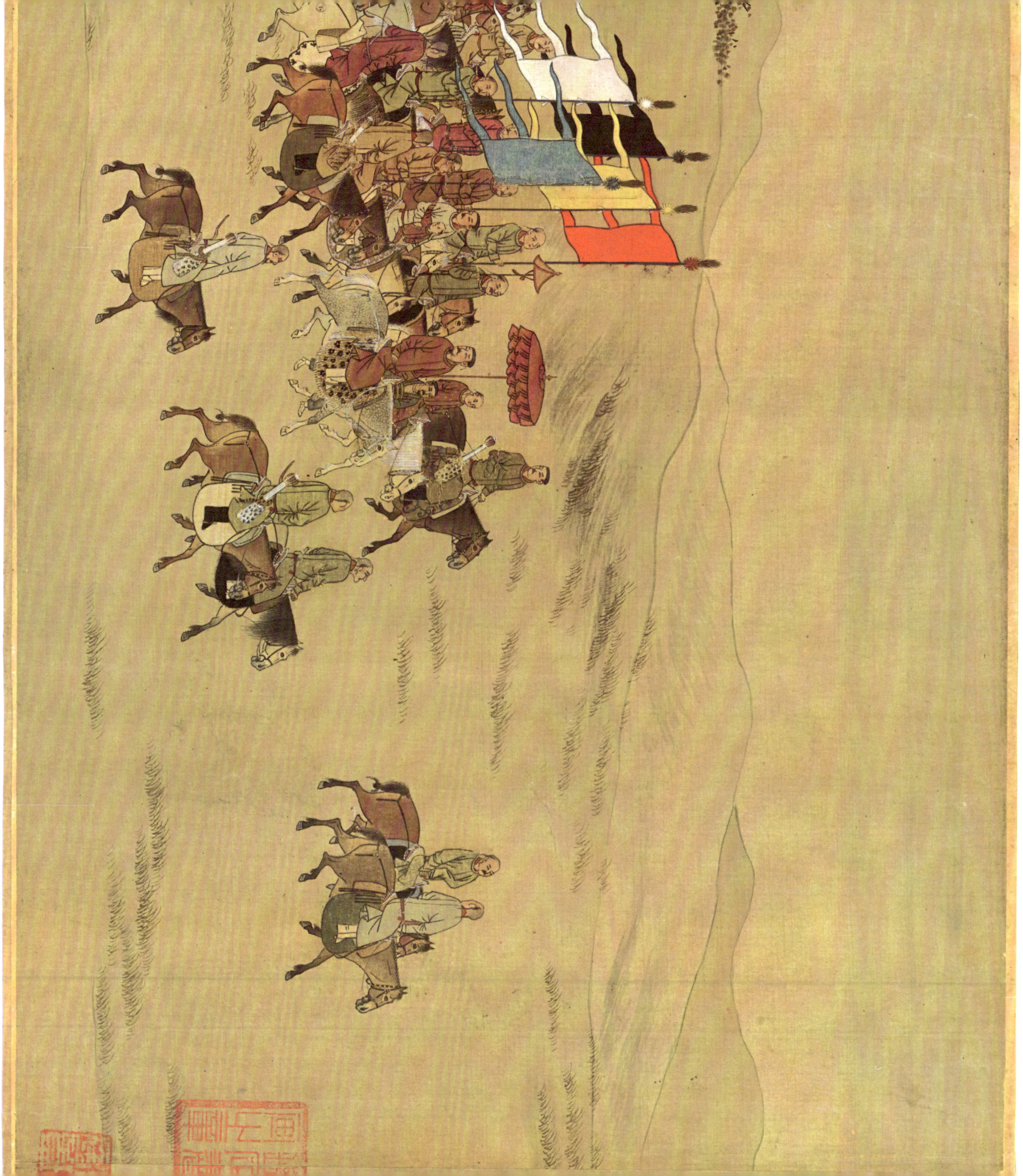

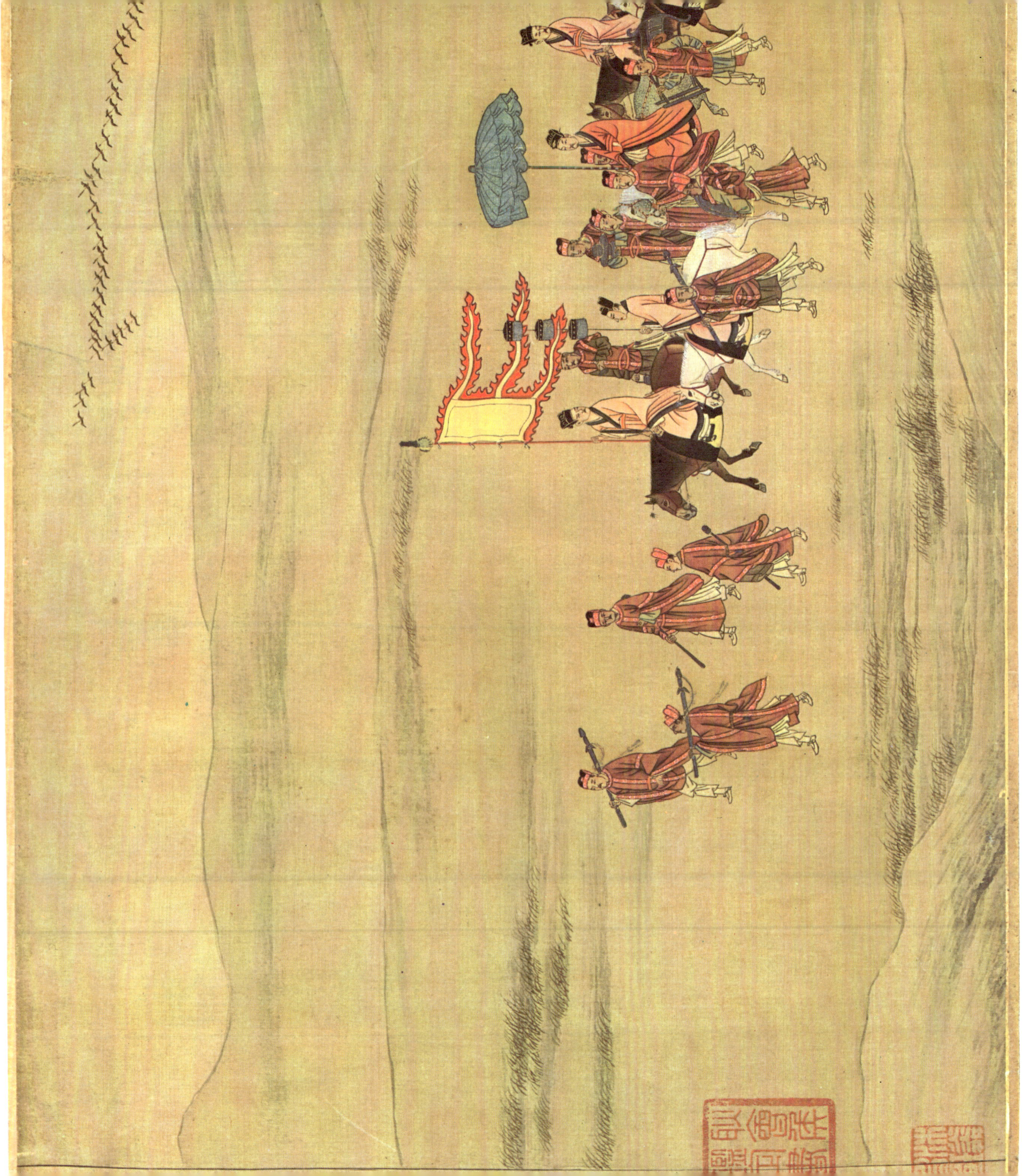

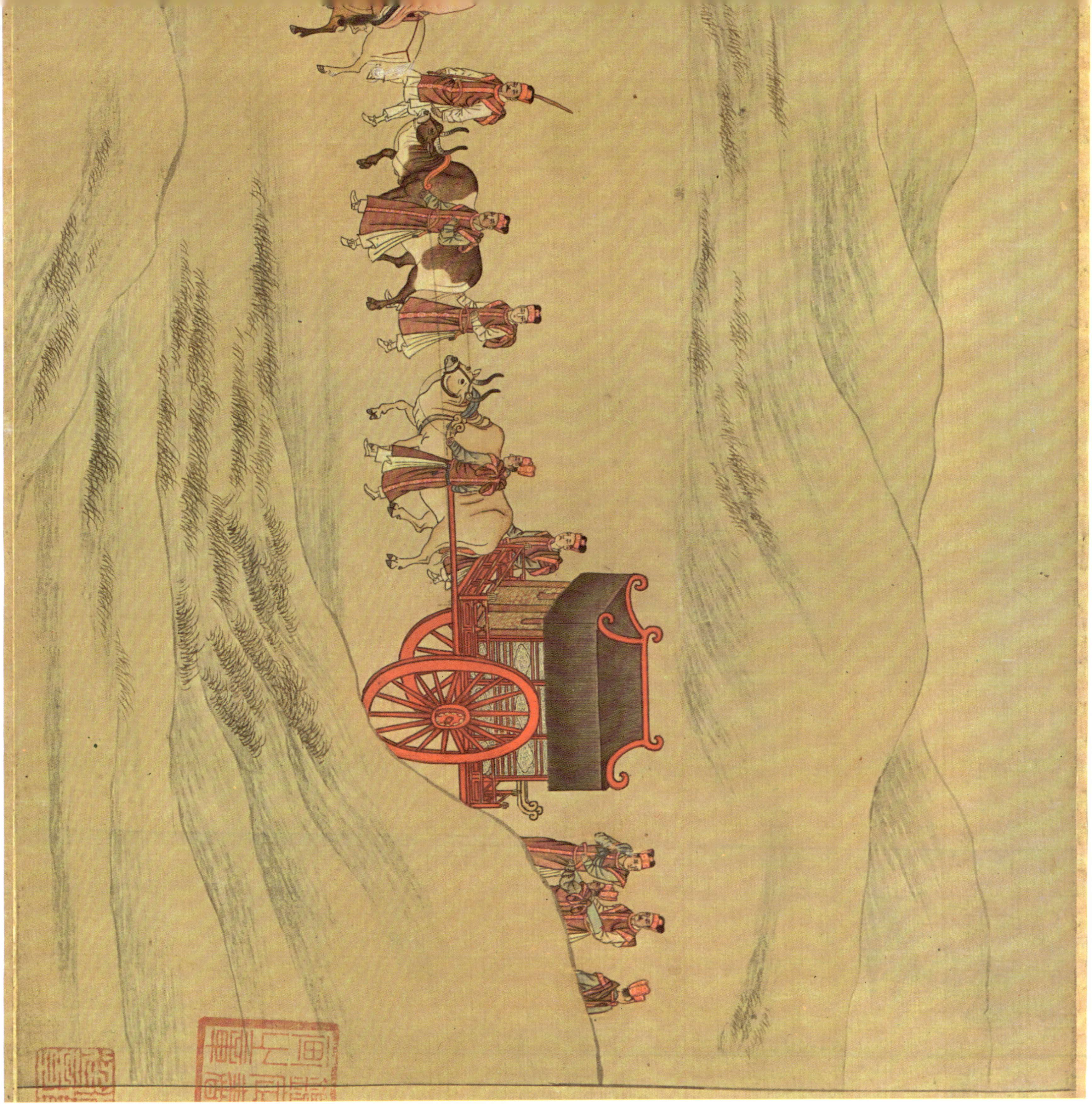

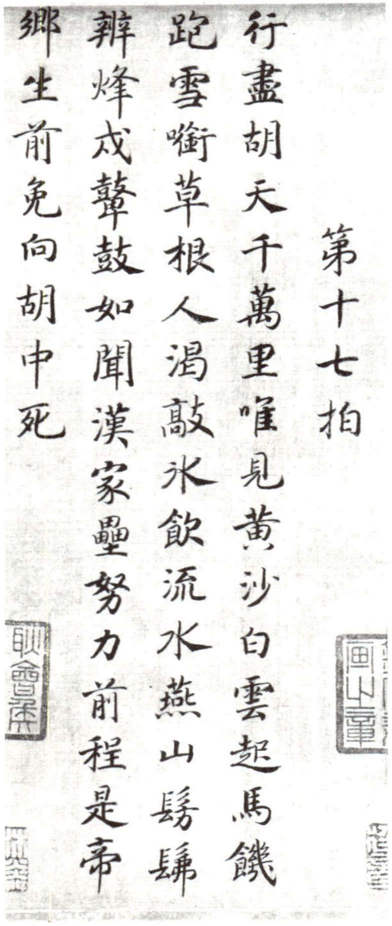

第十七拍
行盡胡天千萬里唯見黃沙白雲起馬饑
跑雪銜草根人渴敲冰飲流水燕山髣髴
辨烽戍鼙鼓如聞漢家壘努力前程是帝
鄉生前免向胡中死

17 A Chinese City in View

We traversed thousands of miles under the nomads' sky,
Seeing only yellow sands and white clouds rising.
The horses are starving; they race across the snow to feed on grass roots.
The men are thirsty; they break through the ice in order to drink the running water.
At Yen-shan we begin to see bonfires and the garrison;*
The sound of military drums tells us that we are hearing the forts of China.
We rally and make our way, assured that the Emperor's land lies ahead.
Life lies ahead, and I have escaped death among the nomads.

* In the north of modern Hopei province. The name is associated with the defense of the Han against the Huns.

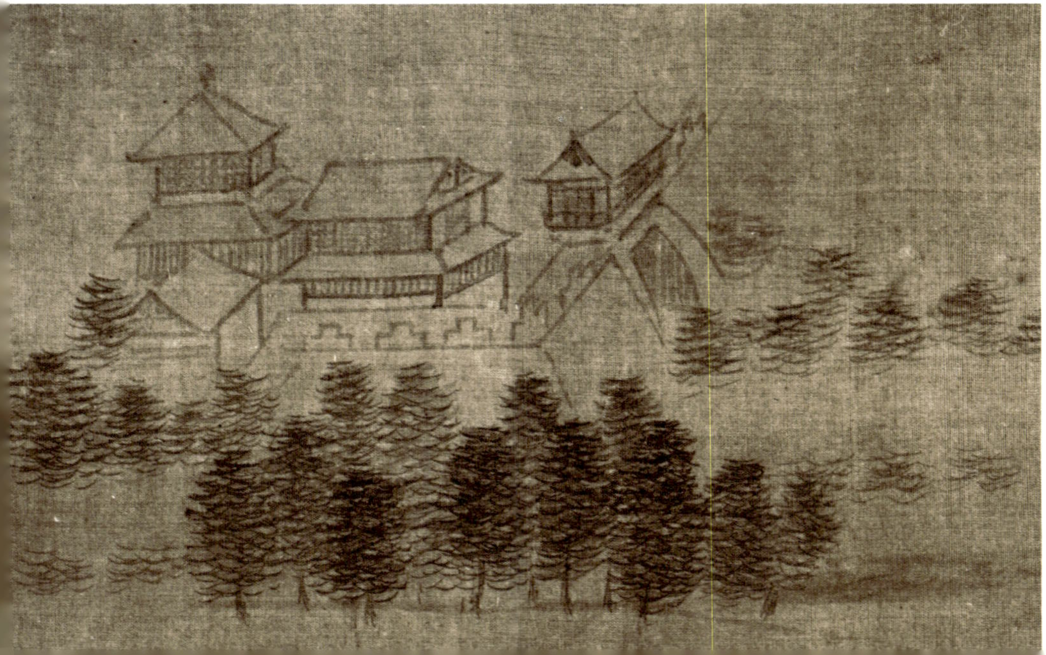

Wen-chi remains secluded in the cart while the troop rests. The landscape closely resembles that of the second scene. The envoy relaxes in his chair. His official staff and the imperial banner are planted in the ground. Far off, indistinct in the winter mist, is a Chinese outpost.

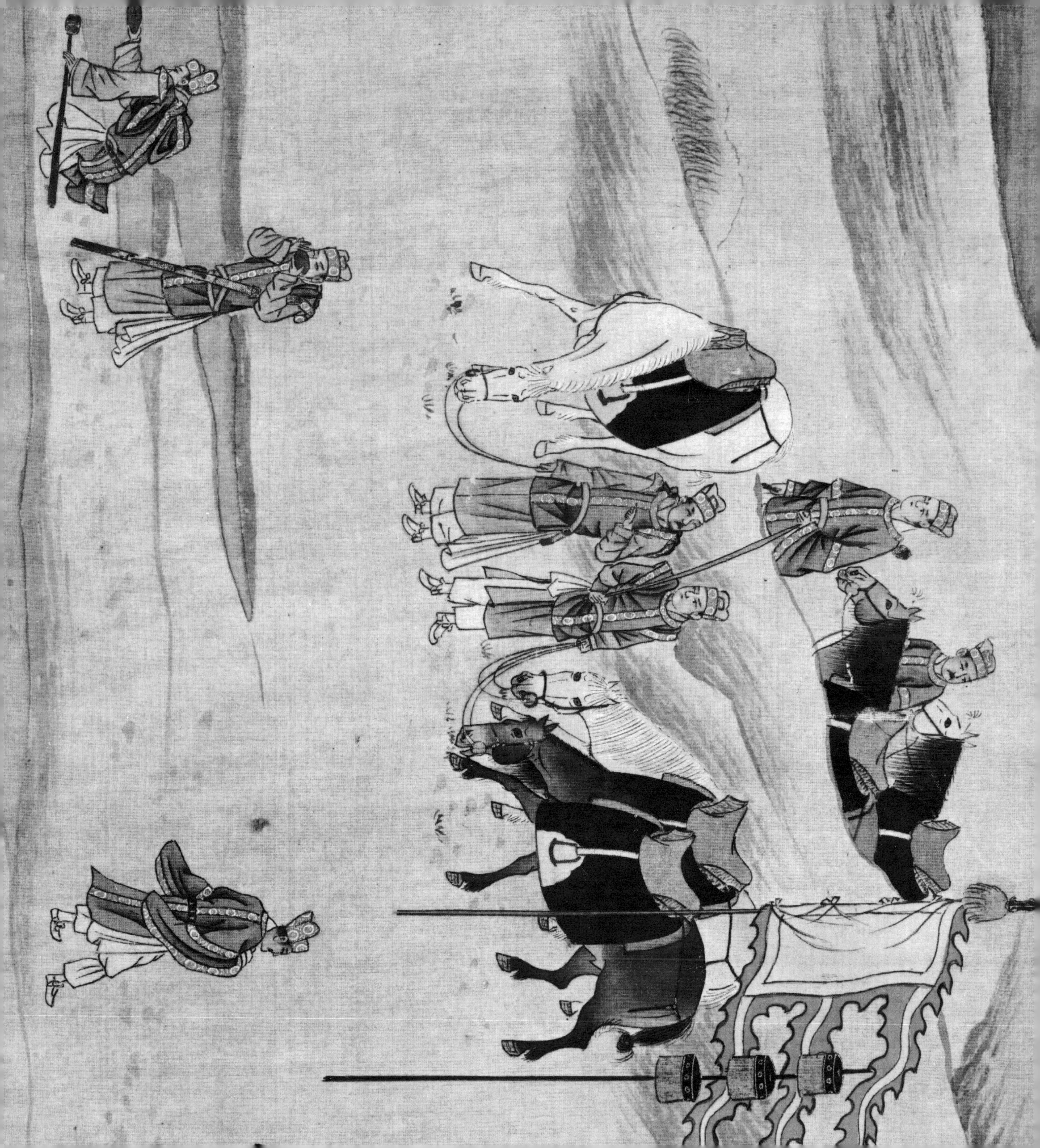

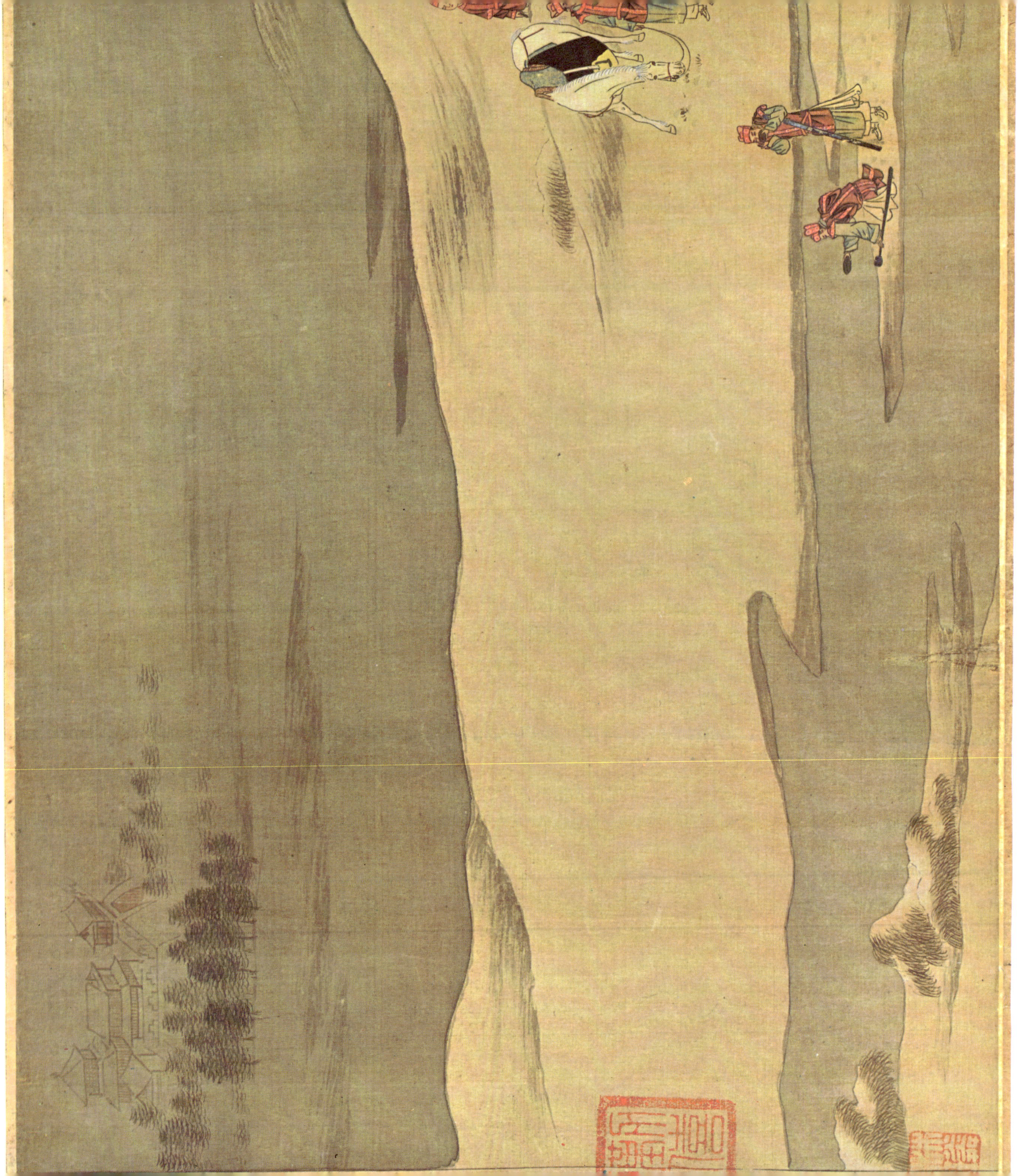

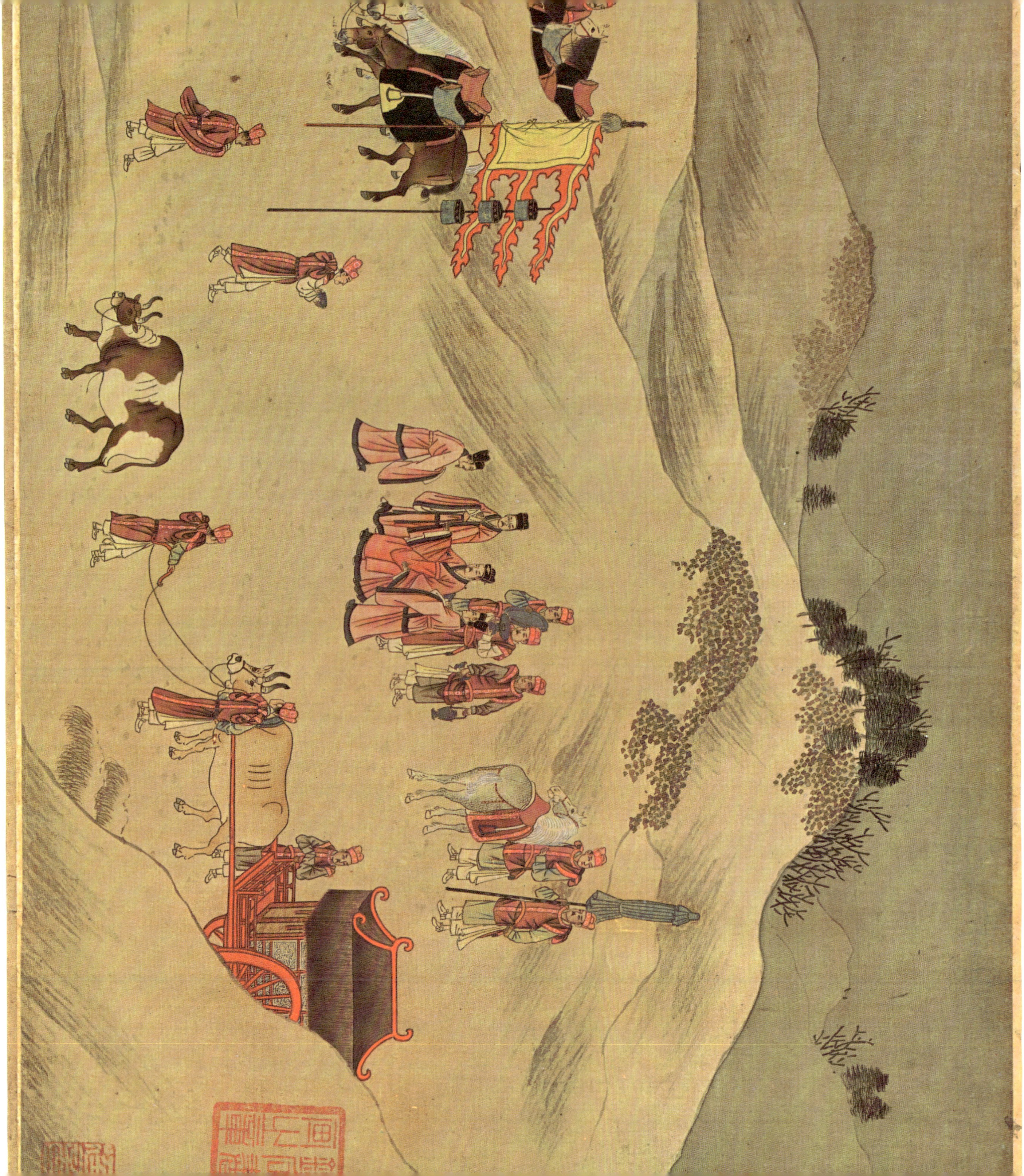

18 Wen-chi Returns Home

I return home and see my kin;
The fields and gardens are half wild, but the spring grass is green.
Bright candles are lit again from ashes and ruins;
Cool spring water cleanses a jade that had sunk in the mire.
As I hold towel and comb, I rediscover the good rituals and etiquettes;
Touching the ch'in again enables me to live or die without regret.
From going out through the pass to my return was twelve years;
Now all my sorrows are told in this Song of the Nomad Flute.

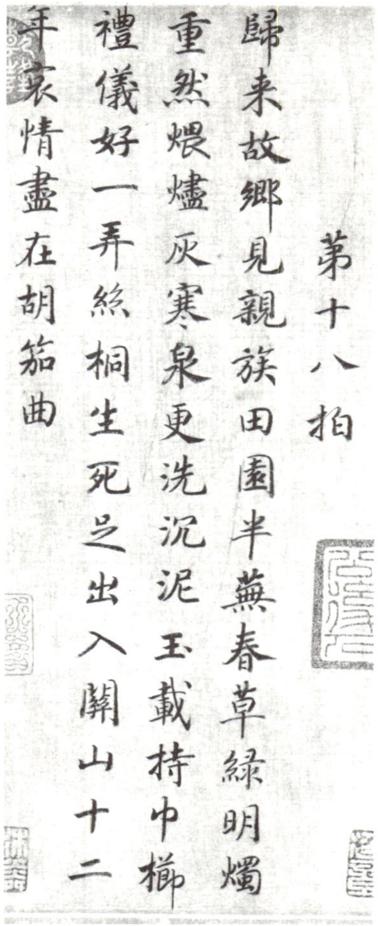

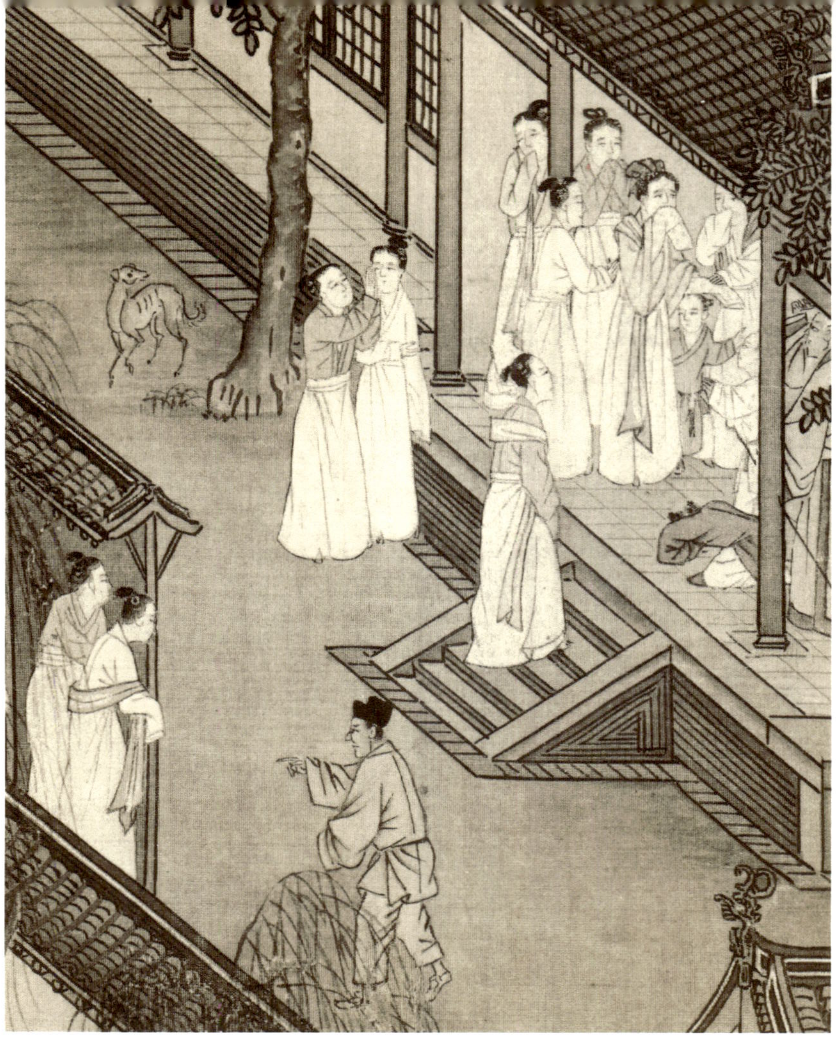

The physical setting is that of the first scene, but the atmosphere and action are very different. Beneath the greening willows the street is abustle: parents with children pass, friends greet and congratulate one another, a young vendor with a box on his back and a clapper in his hand is part of the crowd, as is a man carrying firewood and a scholar with his attendants. A teashop, shuttered against the violence in the first scene, is open. The weary men of the envoy's mission rest along the wall; two of them are buying from a seller of breads. Servants carry Wen-chi's belongings through the gate and withindoors. So long away, Wen-chi, once more dressed as a Chinese lady, walks up the steps to her chambers. Her relatives and friends, sleeves at mouths, endeavor to conceal at least some of their mixed joy and anguish, lest it become unseemly.

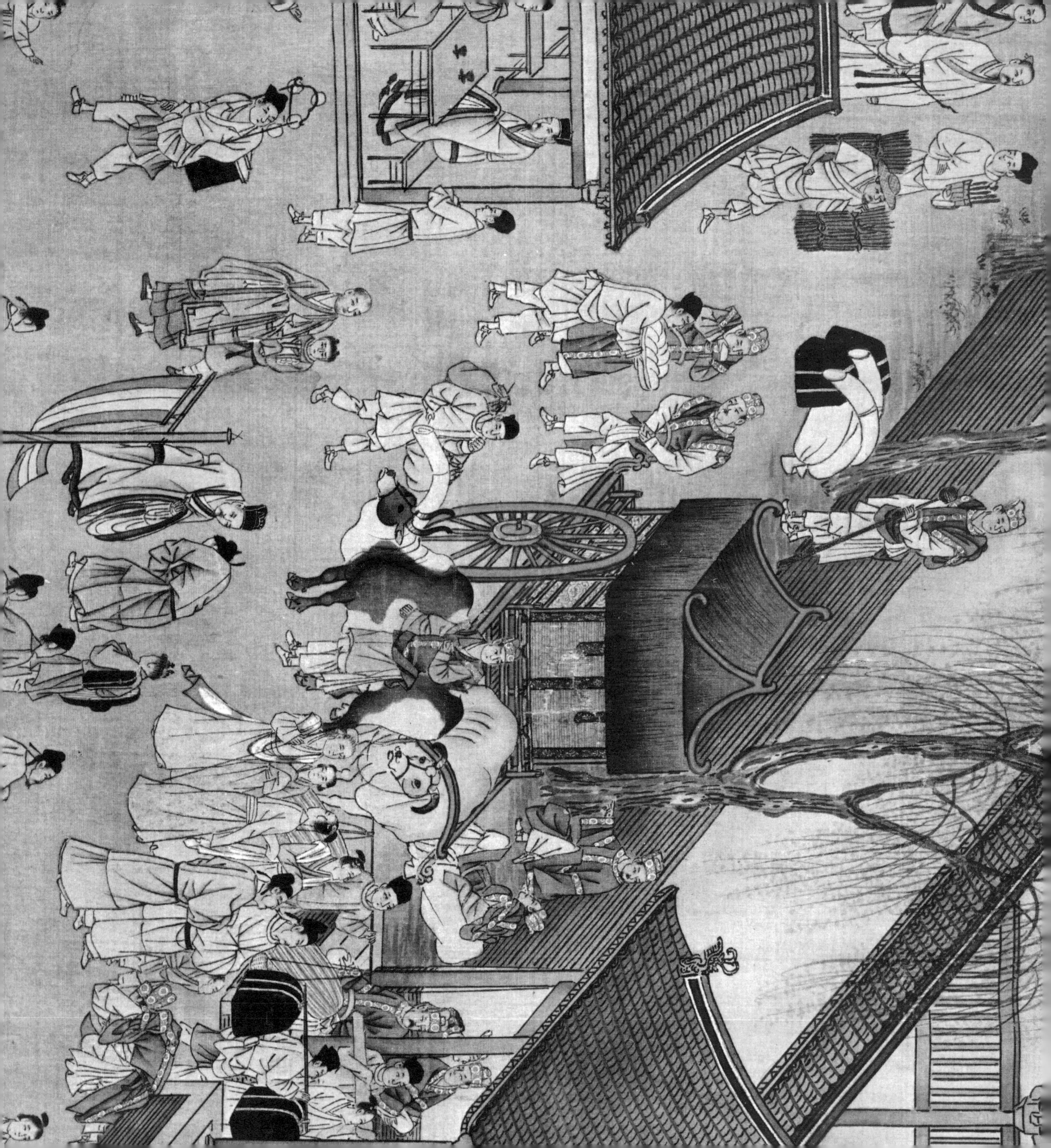

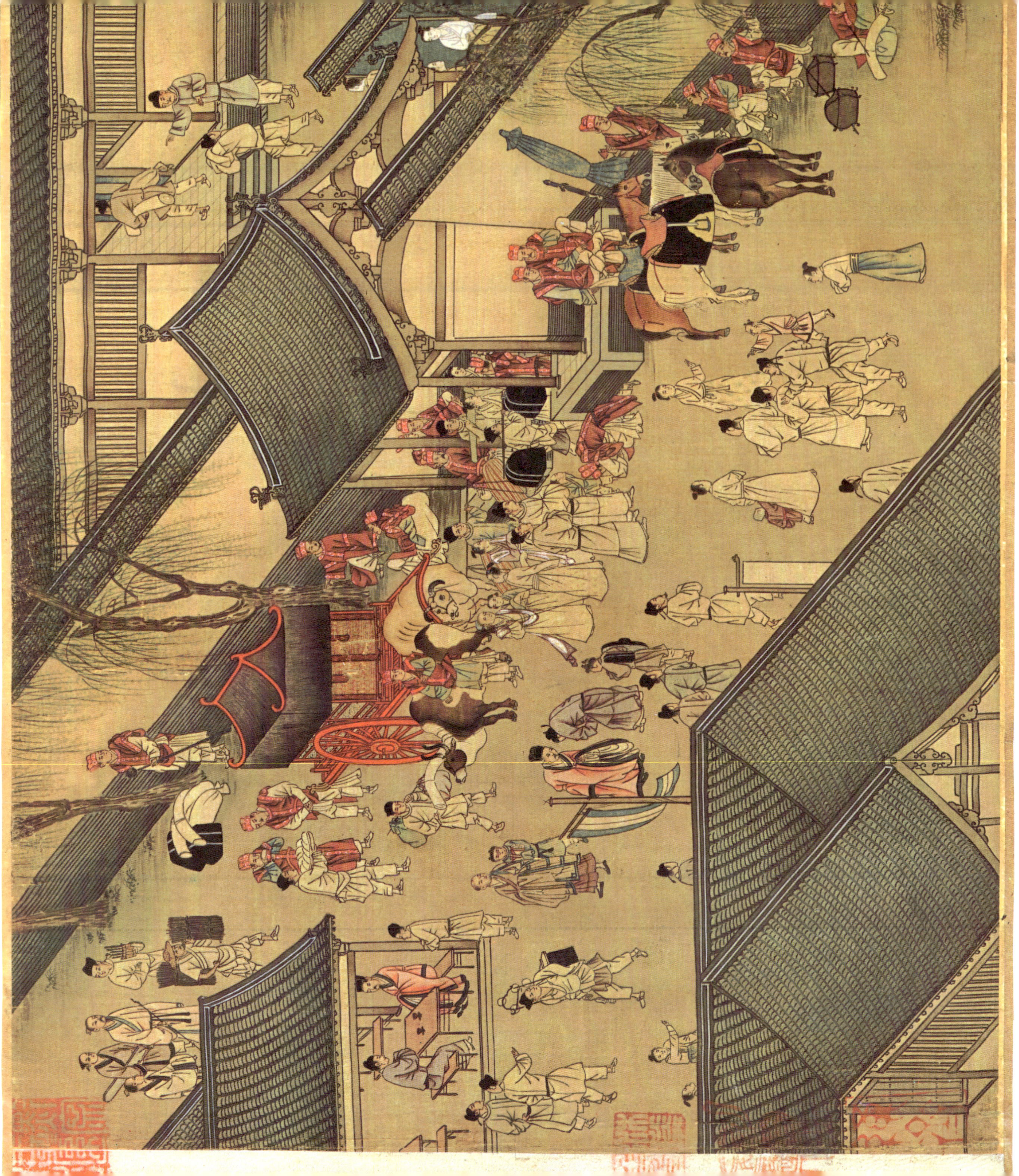

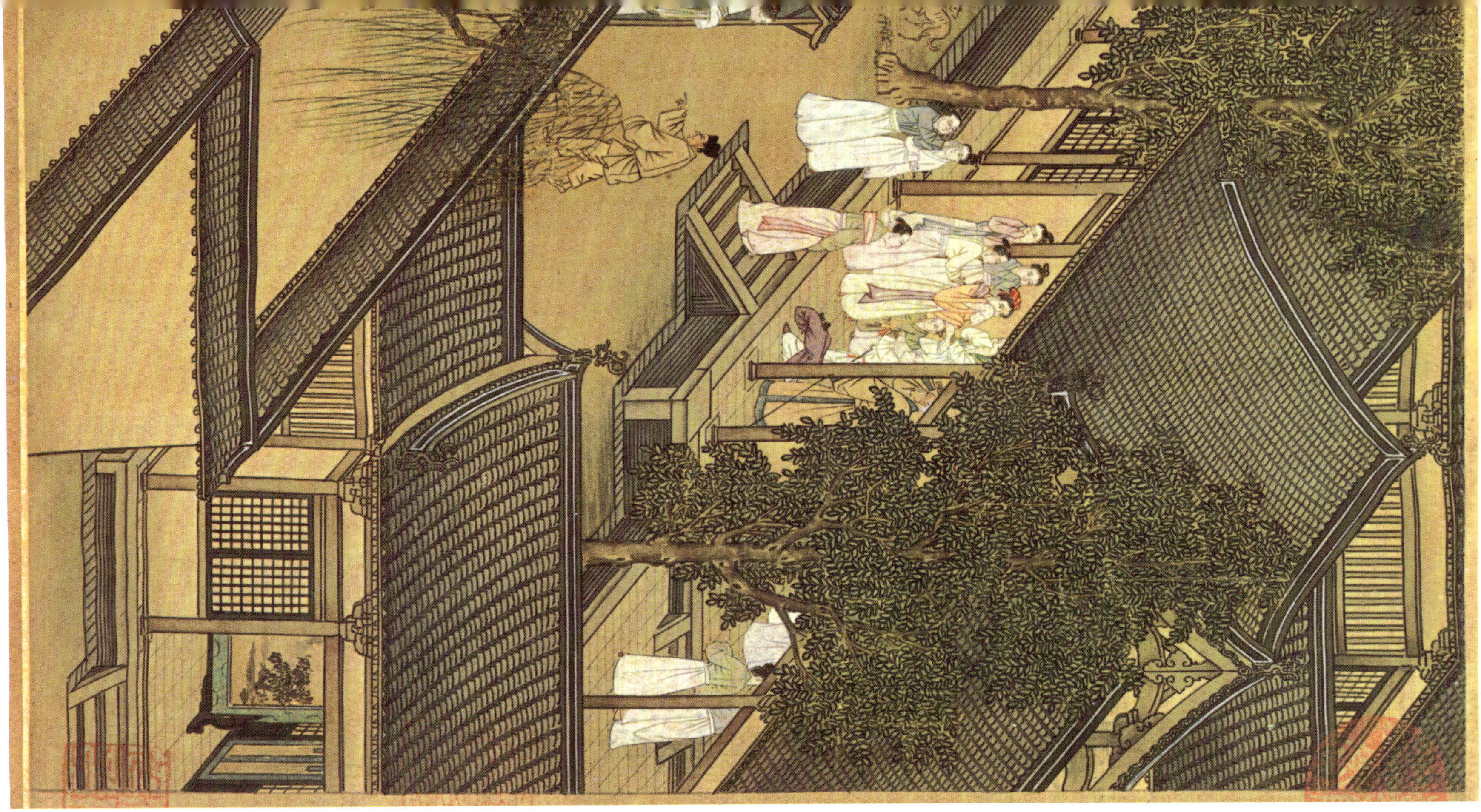

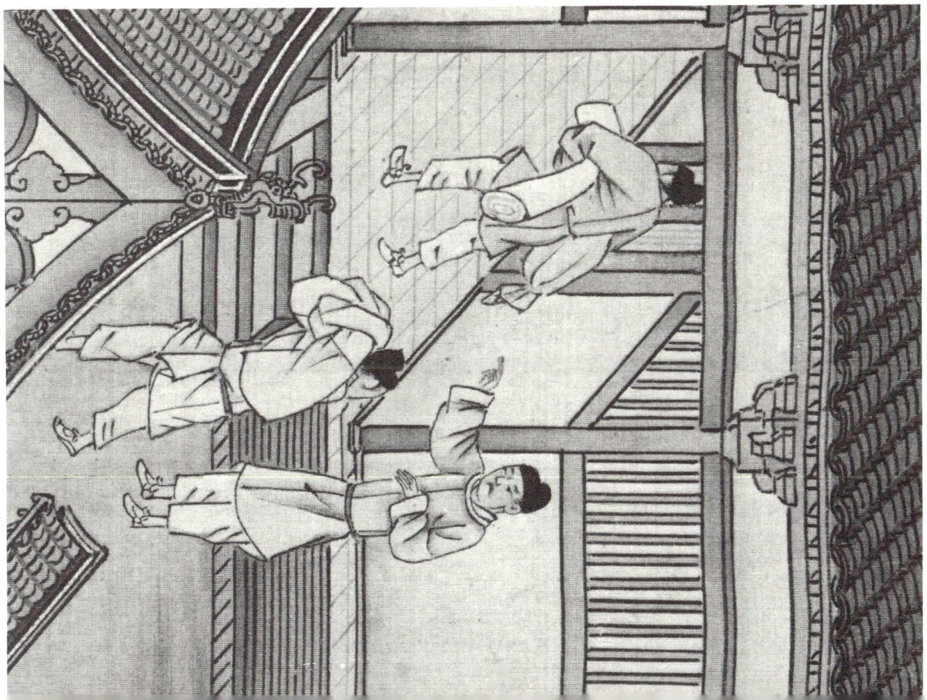

胡笳十八拍

Designed by Peter Oldenburg
Composition by Finn Typographic Service
Color separations by Rainbows
Black-and-white photography and printing by The Meriden Gravure Company
Bound by A. Horowitz & Son